H H STEPHENSO

A Cricketing Journey:
Kennington Oval to Uppingham School

Bust of H H Stephenson
Sculpted by F J Williamson, Esher, 1863

J. S. Dalley
Great Grandson

Roy Stephenson

Roy Stephenson

Supported by Uppingham Local History Study Group

November 2009

© Roy Stephenson

2009

ISBN 978-0-9540076-6-9

Published by Uppingham Local History Study Group

In association with

Roy Stephenson
7 Newtown Road
Uppingham
Rutland
LE15 9TR

Previous Publications of Uppingham Local History Study Group:

Uppingham in 1851: A Night in the Life of a Thriving Town, 2001

Uppingham in 1802, 2002

The Making of Uppingham, 2003

Uppingham in Living Memory: Snapshots of Uppingham in the 20th Century
Part I: Uppingham at War, 2005
Part II: Uppingham in Peacetime, 2007

This publication was edited by Henry Dawe, designed by Lorna Vibert
and printed by Century Print of Cavendish Court, Corby.

CONTENTS

ACKNOWLEDGEMENTS

This publication would not have been possible without the help that I have received from Peter Wynne-Thomas, the Archivist and Librarian for Nottinghamshire County Cricket Club. He has been a tower of strength, unfailingly obliging and courteous, and he willingly placed at my disposal the relevant documents in the library at Trent Bridge.

Writing this biography has given me the opportunity to share with others some of H H Stephenson's personal letters and photographs which are now in the possession of his great-grandson, John Oakley. I am deeply indebted to John and his wife Pat for allowing me full access to this wonderful archive of material and granting me permission to reproduce so many items. Unless otherwise stated, all photographic material and personal items are reproduced by kind permission of John Oakley.

The Uppingham Local History Study Group has supported me in this venture and I must thank Julia Culshaw, Betty Howard, Peter Lane and Margaret Stacey for their contributions. I acknowledge information received from Robin Hunt and John Seaton, not forgetting assistance from the late Peter Scott and my school friend, the late Paul Williams.

I extend my thanks to Harry Spry-Leverton, Uppingham School Librarian, and Jerry Rudman, Uppingham School Archivist, for providing access to the school's archive material, whilst David Ashworth, President of Uppingham Rovers Cricket Club, has provided an invaluable insight into 'The Doings' of that illustrious band of men. Janet Booth, Rossall School Archivist, has also helped me greatly in my research.

I am grateful for information received from Neil Robinson of the M C C Library, Jo Miller, Members' Liaison Officer at Surrey County Cricket Club, Trevor Jones, a former archivist at Surrey County Cricket Club, Graham Ashton of Thames Ditton Cricket Club, Dr Robert Shaw of Evesham Cricket Club, Charles Scott of Uppingham Town Cricket Club, Paul Langton, Secretary of the Esher & District Local History Society and Graham Fisher of Chipping Campden.

The courtesy and cooperation afforded me by staff at the following libraries have been much appreciated: Bridlington Library, Evesham Library, Stamford Library, Surrey History Centre, The British Library Newspapers, The Record Office for Leicestershire, Leicester & Rutland and Worcestershire Library and History Centre. Philippa Bassett, Senior Archivist at the University of Birmingham, also deserves thanks for her detailed research on my behalf.

Finally, I express my sincere thanks to my wife, Claire, for her constant support and encouragement, and for providing me with the motivation to complete this biography.

INTRODUCTION

The life of Heathfield Harman Stephenson spanned the reign of Queen Victoria, a period in our history which witnessed enormous industrial and social reform. The advent of the railway revolutionised travel and communication and was a catalyst for the spread of cricket in the 1850s and 1860s, as it enabled both amateur and professional players to move more easily from one venue to another.

Europe in 1848 saw a wave of uprisings, especially in France where the object of the revolutionary mobs was to obtain a constitutional government. A Republic was proclaimed and the French royal family sought exile in England, where they were welcomed as friends by Queen Victoria and the residents of a small town in Surrey.

In these days of political unrest, the Great Exhibition at the Crystal Palace represented an occasion for nations to come together in peace, as manufacturers and inventors displayed their talent and industry on a grand scale. Meanwhile, on the other side of the world, gold was being discovered at Bathurst, New South Wales.

It is against this background of social and political change that H H Stephenson lived his early years. He overcame the loss of his father to blossom as an all-round cricketer and become one of the finest players of his time, later leading a pioneering team to Australia. The shifting social and political climate impacted upon him and charted the course of his life.

His first-class career over, Stephenson devoted himself to developing the cricketing talents of the boys at Uppingham School, where he was highly respected and revered as a true gentleman and an outstanding cricket coach. Several Old Boys went on to gain a Blue at Oxford or Cambridge and a few later represented their country, inspired by the coaching they had received from the man they affectionately knew as 'H H'.

The aim in writing this biography is to share with cricket enthusiasts and local historians alike the various aspects of H H Stephenson's life which brought him to public prominence and secured him a place in cricketing history.

A Relique

OF

The Princess Charlotte Augusta,

or

A SELECTION of PSALMS and HYMNS

With the appropriate Tunes,

being

An Exact Copy

OF THE GENUINE HYMN BOOK,

used jointly by

The late Princess Charlotte

and Prince Leopold of Saxe Cobourg,

At Public Worship

In the Parish Church of Esher,

near CLAREMONT.

Drawn by W.G. Moss. Engraved by Owen.

South West View of Esher Church, Surrey.

LONDON:

PUBLISHED BY R. MILLER 24 OLD FISH ST DOCTORS COMMONS, & 126 NEWGATE ST FACING SKINNER ST AND SOLD BY J. ARLISS, 38 NEWGATE ST & R. HILL, HIGH ST BOROUGH.

1818.

1. ESHER

This opening chapter examines the historic nature of H H Stephenson's home town of Esher, Surrey, and considers how the exile of the French royal family to the nearby stately home of Claremont shaped a significant part of his life.

Family circumstances

Heathfield Harman Stephenson (henceforth referred to as H H) was born in Esher on 3 May 1833 and was baptised there on 9 October 1834.[1] His sister Rose was born two years later, but tragedy struck the family in 1839 when their father, Charles Thomas Stephenson, a surgeon, died on 13 July of apoplexy.[2]

The 1841 Census indicates that the two children were living with their mother, Catherine Stephenson, then 37 years of age, on Arbrook Common in the parish of Esher. At that time the town had a population of 1,261 people – 596 males and 665 females – and of these just over 100 were described as agricultural labourers.[3]

At the time of the 1851 Census H H was still living at home with his mother and their house servant, Mary Ann Brittle, 42 years of age.[4] In an interview from 1895 H H said: 'In fact my first attempts [to play cricket] were made before I went to school. My mother had a servant who could bowl round arm and play cricket very well. She used to annoy me greatly because she could bowl me out, whereas I could never beat her. When I was at school at Esher, my headmaster was umpiring in a match which we were playing against another boys' team. After I had been bowling for some time he said to me, "Stephenson, you don't ask for l.b.w.

By-the-bye, Stephenson, there will be sixpence for you for every wicket you get." I made half-a-crown out of the match. All the five wickets were l.b.w.'[5]

Esher and surrounding area

In the early part of the 19th century the area around Esher was made up of commons and parkland, with farming and market gardening important occupations. The commons served to separate the various parishes such as Claygate, Thames Ditton (with a population of 1,256)[6] and Esher.

Esher's prosperity was largely dependent on its fine houses, and it could pride itself on the several manor houses situated around the town. It was divided into great estates and the landowners lived in large mansions hidden away in wooded parks. The people in these grand houses tended to regulate the pace of change.

Some of the landowners were rich London merchants, but Mr Martineau of Littleworth House was a barrister and Justice of the Peace.

Artists and writers came to live or stay in Esher. Lady Byron took up residence in Moore House in 1841 in order to be close to her daughter, the Countess of Lovelace, at Sandown House.[7]

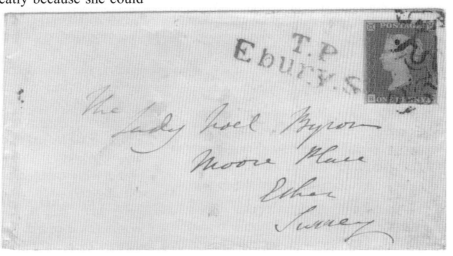

A letter to Lady Byron posted in London on 11 November 1842
From author's collection

Claremont

Claremont and its royal connections

It was with one of the town's stately homes, Claremont, to the south of Esher, that H H came to have a close connection. The first house was built between 1708 and 1714 by Sir John Vanbrugh, the playwright and architect of Blenheim Palace, Stowe and Castle Howard. He sold it in 1714 to Thomas Pelham, who was then known as the Earl of Clare, hence the name Claremont. The house was to change owners several times over the next hundred years, before it was bought by the Crown in 1816 as a residence for the Princess Charlotte, daughter of George IV, upon her marriage to Prince Leopold of Saxe Cobourg.[8]

Sadly, Princess Charlotte passed away on 6 November 1817 following the stillbirth of her child. Having been elected King of the Belgians in 1830, Prince Leopold remarried the following year. His bride was Princesse Louise d'Orléans, daughter of the King and Queen of France. Meanwhile Prince Leopold retained ownership of Claremont and lent it firstly to the Duke and Duchess of Kent and then to their daughter, Princess Victoria.

Exile of the French Royal Family

Uprisings in February 1848 on the streets of Paris led to the overthrow of the monarchy in France, the proclamation of a Republic and the installation of a provisional government. Despite the attack on the Palais Royal, the King and Queen of France managed to escape, assuming the titles of the Comte and Comtesse de Neuilly, and they crossed the Channel to Newhaven. From here they travelled by special train to London and thence by carriage to Claremont which had been put at their disposal by Queen Victoria.

On 23 March 1848, *The Times* reported that the Prince de Joinville and the Duc d'Aumale, who were the sons of the Comte and Comtesse de Neuilly, had arrived together with their wives at Dartmouth from Lisbon and departed for Claremont. They joined the Duc and Duchesse de Nemours with their two sons and daughter and the Duc and Duchesse de Montpensier.[9] The widowed Duchesse d'Orléans and her son, the Comte de Paris, went to live in Moore Place, Esher, by invitation of Lady Byron.

4

Sadly the ex-King, Louis-Philippe, did not enjoy the peace of Claremont for long as he passed away in August 1850, aged 76 years. His widow, Marie-Amélie, indulged in her favourite pastime of hunting, and she continued living there until her death in March 1866.[10]

During this time the Duc and Duchesse d'Aumale lived in Twickenham at Orléans House, where they entertained in a regal manner. They also resided for part of the time on the Claremont estate. Cricket being a seasonal activity, H H was able to occupy himself during the winter months by serving the Duc d'Aumale as a huntsman there. He had a passion for field sports throughout his life and proved an asset to the Duc in this capacity. H H's obliging and courteous behaviour endeared him to the French royal family and he enjoyed a happy association with them for the next 20 years.

The Duc de Nemours

The Prince de Joinville

Conclusion

Its large houses and secluded estates together with its royal associations made Esher a very attractive town in the first part of the 19th century. In his employ with the Duc d'Aumale H H Stephenson held a privileged position; his observation of the style of living in such a household was to prove beneficial to him in later years.

[1] *International Genealogical Index Website*
[2] Certified Copy of Death Certificate of Charles Thomas Stephenson, in author's possession
[3] 1841 Census, Surrey History Centre
[4] 1851 Census, Surrey History Centre
[5] *The Cricket Field*, 1 June 1895, p.142
[6] 1841 Census, Surrey History Centre
[7] Anderson, Ian G, *History of Esher*, The Wolsey Press, Esher, 1948, p.108
[8] Jones, Mrs Herbert, *The Princess Charlotte of Wales*, Bernard Quaritch, London, 1885, pp.130-3
[9] *The Times*, 23 March 1848
[10] Hutchins, Lisa, *Esher and Claygate Past*, Historical Publications Ltd., London, 2001, p.64

2. THE COUNTY CLUB OF SURREY

A brief outline of the official formation of Surrey County Cricket Club precedes an account of the early years of H H Stephenson's career as a professional cricketer.

Early cricketing initiatives in Surrey

Cricket was being played quite extensively in the county in the 18th century and occasionally a side would call itself 'Surrey'. As early as 1730 a match had been played between Surrey and Middlesex on Richmond Green when eleven players from a particular area within these counties adopted the name of their county.[1] This early interest in the game in Surrey came from the patronage that it received from wealthy and influential members of the landed aristocracy and nobility such as the Prince of Wales and Lord Winchilsea.[2]

The fortunes of Surrey declined in the early part of the 19th century; there was no county ground where the club could play its

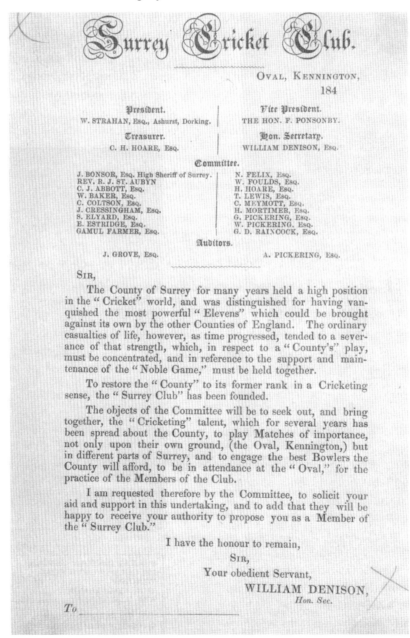

Reproduced by kind permission of Surrey History Centre (ref. 2042/1/1)

6

matches and it became difficult to attract players. However, permission was granted for the conversion of a market garden in Kennington, called The Oval, into a cricket ground in 1845.

Formation of the Surrey Club

That year a match was played between the Gentlemen of Surrey and the Players of Surrey with the object of setting up a new club. The ground 'was accessible by omnibus or by steam from all parts of the metropolis, in about a twenty minutes ride.'[3] A meeting was held on 18 October 1845 to propose the rules by which the club should be governed. It was agreed that the Surrey Club should play its matches at Kennington Oval and that 'an annual subscription of £2 shall entitle a member to every privilege the club affords; that yearly subscribers of £1 shall be entitled to every privilege except

There were few cricket fixtures in these early days. Financial problems, together with disputes over the use of the ground, eventually led to the departure of W Houghton, who had been managing the ground. The lease was handed over and gradually the club acquired complete control of the ground. Under the able management of Mr John Burrup, the club secretary from 1848 until 1855, the Surrey Club slowly began to prosper. He was succeeded as secretary by his twin brother, Mr William Burrup, a wealthy London businessman, whose tremendous enthusiasm spread throughout the club and was a factor in the team's success on the field.[5]

Initially there was no pavilion on the Surrey ground; tents were pitched for the players and there was a single row of spectators. It was only in 1857 that agreement was reached for a pavilion to be built.

SURREY CRICKET-GROUND (1848).
FROM AN ENGRAVING BY C. ROSENBERG.

From the Collection of Mr A. J. Gaston, Brighton.

that of club practice; that the committee of management shall have the power to engage as many practice bowlers and boys to be in attendance upon the ground as they shall think fit.'[4]

Making his debut for Surrey

In his younger days H H played cricket for several clubs in the area around Esher. Throughout his playing career he maintained a close association with Thames Ditton

Cricket Club, which has played on Giggs Hill Green since at least 1833. In the 1860s he often went to Giggs Hill for cricket practice.[6] The club's subscription book for 1879 gives his name and shows that he paid a subscription of five shillings. Sadly, however, an entry in one of the Minute Books for around 1882 notes that the club's records had been lost during the previous decade.[7]

On 4 July 1853 H H played with some distinction for Chertsey against Dorking, making the highest score of 29 and then claiming three stumpings in the match. Later that year he played for Godalming against Shillinglee.

Having been noticed by Mr F P Miller, the Surrey captain, and Mr Charles Hoare, H H was invited to play in a benefit match for Tom Mortlock, Sen. at Kennington Oval. The following day, 29 August 1853, he made his debut for Surrey against Kent, deputising for wicket-keeper Tom Lockyer, who was injured. It was a satisfactory match for him as he was responsible for one catch and one stumping, and then he scored 13 runs in all for just one dismissal.

First full season

The 1854 season saw H H playing in matches for Reigate, Godalming, Chertsey, Upton Park and then West Wickham in Kent, whilst 15 'Odds' matches for the All England Eleven were interspersed with seven first-class matches. The latter comprised four county fixtures for Surrey, one for Surrey Club, one for the South of England and finally selection for England in a match arranged by William Clarke.

In his first full season as a professional cricketer H H made an immediate impression, putting in some outstanding performances with the ball. Playing for Surrey against Nottinghamshire at Trent Bridge in July, he achieved match figures of 50-24-55-10, which included an analysis of 10-6-4-4 in the first innings. With only four balls in an over in those days, this still represents a very accurate and economical spell of bowling. With his innings of 28 and

21, H H was certainly a major contributor to Surrey's victory by 97 runs.

He followed these figures with another devastating performance, this time playing for England against Sussex in mid-August at Hove. In the Sussex first innings his bowling figures were 18-8-22-7, with six of his victims being clean bowled.

That season, in seven first-class matches, H H claimed 43 wickets at an average of 8.19, a superb achievement in his first year as a professional; of these 43 dismissals 28 were clean bowled. Another notable feat is that H H succeeded in dismissing the formidable batsman George Parr five times in the four matches when they were on opposing sides.

A fellow professional, William Caffyn, was fulsome in his praise of H H: 'As a bowler he was a genius. He bowled rather fast, with a tremendous break from the off. Indeed we may almost look upon Stephenson as the pioneer of break-back round-arm bowling. As a bowler he had his good days and bad. Sometimes he would bowl in a manner that was almost unplayable, whilst at another he would seem to lose his command over the pitch of the ball. For a few seasons he was, in my opinion, about the most difficult bowler in England.'[8]

Because of the dispute with the owner Surrey did not play any matches at Kennington Oval in 1854. Their only game in Surrey took place at Broadwater Park in Godalming, whilst one away fixture was played at Trent Bridge and two matches were played against Sussex at Hove. The match at Hove at the end of June was regarded as the most exciting inter-county contest of 1854: the correspondent in *Bell's Life* noted that he could not do justice 'to the brilliant display of cricket exhibited throughout the three days.'[9]

Payment

At a committee meeting of the Surrey Club held on 28 April 1853 it was agreed 'That in any County match played by the Club the pay of the players engaged shall be as follows:

Groundsmen £2 to lose and £3 to win
Other players £3 to lose and £4 to win

with second-class travelling expenses to be paid for away matches, and for home fixtures should the player come from any place out of the county a greater distance than 50 miles.'[10]

In 1855 H H played in only one match for Surrey. Both Julius Caesar and H H refused to play in the Sussex v Surrey match at Hove on 25 June because of the expense involved in travelling from Manchester. The request for an increase in pay was rejected and they were temporarily excluded from the Surrey team.

As a result H H played in all the 'Odds' matches involving the All England Eleven that year. During one of these fixtures, played at the back of the Half Moon Inn at Bristol, he encountered Dr H M Grace and three of his sons playing for the XXII of West Gloucestershire.

The following year both Julius Caesar and H H were reinstated in the Surrey side. However, as Surrey had only three county matches that year, H H played on 17 occasions for the All England Eleven, mainly as wicket-keeper. In 1857 the trend was slightly reversed as he featured in 18 first-class matches, but only eleven for the All England Eleven. H H recaptured some of his earlier bowling form at Derby against XXII of Derbyshire when he returned the excellent figures of 18-?-14-9 in the first innings and 43-?-55-5 in the second.[11] (The *M C C Cricket Scores and Biographies* presented bowling analyses in terms of balls bowled, with no indication of any maiden overs.)

Southern domination

At this stage in cricket's development very few first-class county matches were being played. In the four years from 1854 until 1857 only 23 county matches were played, involving the counties of Sussex (17), Surrey (14), Kent (10), Cambridgeshire (2), Nottinghamshire (2) and Yorkshire (1).

A significant reason for this lay in the formation of the All England Eleven and the United All England Eleven which involved the main professional cricketers. This development within the game at first restricted but then ultimately accelerated and fostered the creation of county clubs. During these same years, out of a total of 108 first-class cricket matches only ten were played in the north of England.

Conclusion

An auspicious start to his professional career as a bowler brought H H Stephenson to early prominence and recognition within the cricketing world, laying a solid foundation for later success. He became an integral member of the Surrey side, which was to enjoy much success during the next few years.

[1] Lemmon, David, *The Official History of Middlesex County Cricket Club*, Christopher Helm, London, 1988, p.21
[2] Lemmon, David, *The Official History of Surrey County Cricket Club*, Christopher Helm, London, 1989, p.6
[3] *The Sunday Times*, 31 August 1845
[4] *ibid.*, 19 October 1845
[5] Ranjitsinhji, K S, *The Jubilee Book of Cricket*, William Blackwood & Sons, Edinburgh and London, 1897, pp.424-5
[6] Alverstone, Lord and Alcock, C W, *Surrey Cricket – its history and associations*, Longmans, Green and Co., London, 1902, p.431
[7] E-mail communication from Graham Ashton, Thames Ditton Cricket Club, 25 August 2008
[8] Caffyn, William, *Seventy-one not out: the reminiscences of William Caffyn*, William Blackwood & Sons, Edinburgh and London, 1899, p.90
[9] *Bell's Life in London and Sporting Chronicle*, 9 July 1854
[10] Minutes of a committee meeting of the Surrey County Cricket Club, 28 April 1853, Surrey History Centre
[11] *M C C Cricket Scores and Biographies*, vol. V: 1855-1857, Longman and Co., London, 1876, p.393

3. WILLIAM CLARKE AND THE ALL ENGLAND ELEVEN

This chapter deals with the formation of the All England Eleven, its popularity and its financial success which inflamed the resentment of some players towards its manager and led to the creation of the United All England Eleven. It describes the emergence of H H Stephenson in the All England Eleven and his first appearance in Uppingham.

William Clarke and Trent Bridge

In the 1830s William Clarke was landlord of the Bell Inn, which became the headquarters of Nottingham cricket. A reputable batsman and bowler of slow underarm lobs, he became captain of the Nottingham Old Club, playing on the Forest where spectators had free admission. In 1838 he moved from the Bell to the Trent Bridge Inn where, on an adjacent site, he opened a new cricket ground to paying spectators. Initially the venture was not a financial success because of the limited number of important games that could be played at Trent Bridge in a season, so Clarke went to London in 1846 as a professional bowler on the Lord's staff.[1]

An All England Eleven is founded

That same year Clarke set up an All England Eleven with some of the best professional cricketers, and on 31 August 1846 they began a three-day match against Twenty of Sheffield on the Hyde Park Ground. They underestimated the strength of the opposition, however, and the match resulted in defeat by five wickets for the Eleven. Further games that September against Eighteen of Manchester, followed by a game on Woodhouse Moor against Eighteen of Yorkshire, produced convincing victories for the Eleven.

In 1847 the Eleven played ten matches at Leicester, York, Manchester, Birmingham, Liverpool, Sheffield, Leeds, Newcastle upon Tyne, Stockton-on-Tees and Stourbridge with variable success. Three matches were won, three were lost and the remaining four were unfinished. These contests were essentially northern affairs but in 1848

matches were played in Gravesend, Chelmsford and at Itchen near Southampton.

Clarke's aim was to improve the opportunities open to northern professionals. Hitherto it had been impossible to make a living as a professional cricketer, so the formation of a touring team was welcomed by the players. It gave them the opportunity to develop and exploit their cricketing abilities, providing them with some regular money.

To offset the difference in playing ability, the home side usually fielded up to 22 players who included two or three bowlers lent to them by Clarke in order to make the match more even. As Frederick Lillywhite states, 'These encounters soon caused cricket to increase vastly all over England, as being the means (especially in the North) of discovering many fine players, who would never have been "brought out" had they not had the opportunity of first distinguishing themselves against the England Eleven in their visits to different parts.'[2]

THE BOWLER

WILLIAM CLARKE

The Slow Bowler and Secretary to the All England Eleven

The expansion of the railway system together with better roads throughout the country saw a steady increase in the number of matches being played by the All England Eleven. This improvement in travel and communication meant that more towns were becoming accessible to the Eleven, so that interest in cricket soon spread to a wider public. Invitations began to pour in from clubs for the honour of challenging the Eleven. In 1851 the season extended over a period of 22 weeks during which William Caffyn played in over 40 matches. He reflected on the pressures imposed upon the players: 'Playing so many matches was a great strain on one's constitution. We often had to travel all night and begin play at eleven o'clock on the morning we arrived at our place of destination, and I have often been so tired that I have almost fallen asleep while in the field.'[3]

Financial profits lead to resentment and defection

For William Clarke the financial success of the venture was assured, as clubs had to pay around £70 for the privilege of staging the match. Sometimes, though, Clarke would simply accept the gate money in payment. According to William Caffyn, the players were paid £4 for the All England matches, but this could rise to £5 or £6 for a win or an additional allowance for travelling expenses.

Clarke acted in an autocratic and dictatorial manner throughout. On the pitch he would do more than his fair share of the bowling when he sensed that the opposition was weak. Playing at Edgbaston against XXII of Birmingham on 19 and 20 June 1848, he claimed 24 wickets in the match, with John Wisden taking 17 wickets. In financial matters he showed an equally mean streak, and this caused great friction as the players' wages remained virtually the same despite the increased revenue generated by the large crowds. This led to much ill-feeling and resentment among the players at Clarke's lack of generosity towards them. In 1852 the Sussex professionals John Wisden and James Dean set up a rival group called the United All England Eleven who played their

first game at Portsmouth on 26 August 1852, followed by another at Newmarket on 30 August in the presence of William Clarke.

At a meeting held on 7 September 1852 in the Adelphi Hotel, Sheffield, 14 members of this United All England Eleven agreed 'not to play in any match of cricket, for or against, wherein William Clarke may have the management or control (county matches excepted) in consequence of the treatment they have received from him at Newmarket.'[4]

Fortunately key players such as the elderly amateurs Alfred Mynn and Fuller Pilch, together with George Parr, the Nottinghamshire professional, remained loyal to William Clarke. In a positive way the break-up of the original members of the All England Eleven opened the door of opportunity for players such as H H, who made his debut for the team in 1854 at Enville Hall, the Staffordshire seat of the Earl of Stamford.

'Country-house' cricket

For many years the game of cricket had been the preserve of the landed gentry and nobility. It was through playing cricket that the sons of the aristocracy acquired the Victorian qualities of loyalty and self-discipline.

The Earl of Stamford frequently hosted matches at Enville Hall. Educated at Eton and Trinity College, Cambridge, he was elected President of the Marylebone Club in 1851 and each season he employed professional cricketers such as R C Tinley, R Bickley and E Willsher. Visiting teams were entertained most hospitably there, and on one occasion in 1854 'the Hungarian band was in attendance, and the evenings were spent by fireworks on a very large and magnificent scale, causing thousands to leave their homes for miles around.'[5]

In 1854 the All England Eleven were heavily defeated by the Earl of Stamford's Eleven by an innings and 130 runs, and in June 1856 by 15 wickets. Such defeats were becoming a matter of course: 'It is presumed no Eleven could beat such a Twenty-two as that collected by the Earl of Stamford who…had the power of selection of any Gentleman of England he chose to ask, in addition to his own professional players.'[6] In these two matches H H only succeeded in scoring five runs in the four innings, so heavily were the odds stacked against visiting Elevens.

From this place they passed on to...

Uppingham, which, being the first appearance of the Eleven in that neighbourhood, caused great interest. It was somewhat late before the Eleven arrived on the ground, having a cross country to traverse from Enville. The ground is situated on a high hill, commanding extensive views round as fine a grazing country as any in England, as well as Rockingham Castle, the seat of the successors to the celebrated Lord Saunds, who was a patron and supporter of the noble game. For Uppingham, F. Tinley scored 0 and 34, G. Knight 24 and 6, Buttress 12 and 2, H. Hunt 0 and 12, Pearson 0 and 12. England, G. Parr 14 and (not out) 45, Willsher 17 and 3, Caffyn 13 and 3, S. Parr 1 and 18, A. Clarke 12 and (not out) 3. Bowlers—Clarke 392 balls, 70 runs, 24 wickets; Caffyn 311 balls, 71 runs, 17 wickets; Buttress 7 wickets, F. Tinley 9.

Lillywhite, *The Guide to Cricketers*,
Eighth Edition, p.54

So, in 1854, at 21 years of age and in only his second game for the All England Eleven, H H found himself playing at Uppingham which, according to the 1851 Census, had a population of 2,065. At that time there were 63 scholars on roll at Uppingham Grammar School where he was to be employed in later years.

As for the match, it resulted in victory for the Eleven by four wickets, with William Clarke claiming 23 wickets and William Caffyn 17 wickets in the match. Uppingham's team was strengthened by the inclusion of two professional bowlers, William Buttress and Francis Tinley. In the match Tinley claimed 9 wickets and Buttress 7 wickets, which meant that the professional bowlers dominated the match by claiming all the wickets. It is unlikely that any of the Uppingham bowlers were given the opportunity to bowl; for them and the other members of the team it was considered an honour to play against some of the most famous players of the time. William Buttress was regarded as one of the best bowlers of his day but he was rarely selected for important games as he was too fond of drink. On one occasion at Lord's he was found sitting up a tree singing when he was required to bat![7] Officiating as umpires at Uppingham were Thomas Aris, from the

High Street, a 47 year-old watchmaker, and the Kent professional, William Hillyer. This game was played on the area called Van Diemen's Land, situated on the right-hand side along the road to Rockingham, just after the turn to Lyddington.[8]

ALL ENGLAND CRICKET MATCH,
Thursday, Friday, & Saturday, July 13, 14, & 15, 1854.

ALL ENGLAND.

	1st ins.	2nd ins.
Anderson, c Thackeray b Tinley	7	b Tinley 5
A. Clarke, c Dodwell b Buttress	12	not out 3
Caffyn, b Tinley	13	c Pearson b Tinley 3
Cæsar, c Thackeray b Buttress	0	c Thackeray b Tinley 0
Parr, c Tomblin b Buttress	14	not out 45
Guy, b Tinley	0	.. ..
S. Parr, c Knight b Tinley	1	c Bramley b Buttress 18
Box, b Buttress	4	.....
Willsher, c G. Brown b Tinley	17	c Woodcock b Buttress 7
Stephenson, c Woodcock b Buttress	7	c Hawley b Tinley 0
Clarke, not out	0	.....
Byes, 7; leg byes, 2	9	Byes, 3; wide, 3; leg byes, 3 8
Total	**84**	**Total** 89

UPPINGHAM & DISTRICT.

C. Watson, c Anderson, b Clarke	0	c S. Parr b Clarke 4
P. Bramley, b Caffyn	1	c S. Parr b Clarke 5
A. Tomblin, b Caffyn	0	b Clarke 0
E. Hawley, c and b Clarke	3	c Cæsar b Caffyn 0
C. Hart, b Caffyn	4	b Clarke 3
W. H. Brown, b Caffyn	3	c Anderson b Clarke 2
H. Hunt, b Caffyn	0	run out 12
Tinley, c Anderson, b Caffyn	0	c and b Caffyn 34
Pearson, b Clarke	0	c G. Parr b Caffyn 12
G. Knight, c G. Parr b Caffyn	24	a Stevenson b Clarke 6
C. Thackeray, c Anderson b Clarke	3	run out 0
B. Brown, b Caffyn	0	c Caffyn b Clarke 0
S. L. Greaves, s Stephenson b Clarke	0	b Clarke 2
Green, b Clarke	6	b Caffyn 5
G. W. Brown, b Caffyn	2	c Stevenson b Caffyn 0
J. Woodcock, c Box b Clarke	0	c G. Parr b Clarke 1
W. Lee, b Clarke	0	not out 8
Buttress, b Clarke	12	b Clarke 2
J. Brown, b Caffyn	0	b Clarke 0
Dodwell, b Clarke	0	b Caffyn 6
Weston, b Clarke	0	b Clarke 0
C. Ingram, not out	2	d Stephenson b Caffyn 0
Leg Bye	1	Leg byes, 5; no balls, 1 .. 6
Total	**64**	**Total** 108

Umpires—Mr. Hillyer and T. Aris.
PRINTED ON THE GROUND, BY J. HAWTHORN, UPPINGHAM.

Lillywhite's account of the match and this scorecard vary slightly, reflecting the differences that occasionally occur in records at this time.

Excitement and glamour

Glowing reports abound concerning the All England Eleven fixtures; they were eagerly awaited and became a social highlight of the year wherever they were played. Committees were set up to organise the occasion, arrange some form of entertainment and erect marquees on the ground to provide luncheons for players and spectators who would come from miles around on foot or by carriage.

In this respect the Lincolnshire town of Sleaford comes in for special praise from players and commentators alike. The cricket ground was owned originally by the Marquis of Bristol and was part of his large landed estate in the Sleaford area. William Caffyn states: 'This match at Sleaford became an annual thing, and we all looked forward to it with pleasure and left the place with regret.'[9] The match at Sleaford on 11-13 July 1859 was the ninth successive season that a game had been played in this 'spirited little town' where 'the arrangements were on that liberal and extensive scale which has always characterised the management of this committee.'[10]

The social scene at Broughton, Manchester, on 20 July 1854 attracted as much attention as the game itself: 'No one, unless he has had the pleasure of being at Broughton to witness one of these contests, can picture to himself the excitement it creates...More complete accommodation, for the convenience of the public, was never witnessed on any cricket ground, including an ample promenade for the ladies, who, every season, honour the ground with their attendance, and thereby considerably enhance the proceedings. It must be highly gratifying to the executive to find their exertions so well appreciated by the fairer portion of the public, whose elegant dresses, and bright and happy faces, were an evidence of how much they enjoyed the scene around them, as they promenaded to the delightful strains of the fine band of the 3rd Light Dragoons.'[11]

Some outstanding performances

Having made his debut for the All England Eleven at Enville Hall, followed by the game at Uppingham, H H played regularly for the Eleven that season and featured in 15 matches, acting as wicket-keeper in the matches at Uppingham and Maidstone. His major contribution was as a round-arm bowler who took 133 wickets for the Eleven that season. At Broughton Park, he returned figures of 26-14-42-8 in the first innings and in the second innings his analysis of 37-22-31-9 was even more impressive. It is not surprising, therefore, that H H was one of the professionals engaged by Broughton Park as a bowler in 1859. In these 15 matches, however, he only managed to score 157 runs.

Some of the pitches on which the team played were rough and poorly prepared. Sheep were allowed to graze on some grounds in order to keep the grass short, as lawn mowers were not yet in general use. Scores were generally low, there were no boundaries and batsmen had to be especially fit as all scores had to be run. Scoring runs against 22 fielders was never easy and a member of the Eleven had to develop his own technique to overcome the problem, although the opposition was often of an inferior standard.

A single-wicket match

Single-wicket cricket had its own set of rules and had been in existence before the first known eleven-a-side match. It demanded that the batsman keep one foot behind the crease, and a run was scored when the batsman had touched the bowling stump and returned to his crease.[12] By now such encounters had become a rarity, but at the end of the season, on 17 and 18 October 1854, H H joined forces with his friend William Caffyn at Chertsey in Surrey against Julius Caesar and Tom Sherman for the sum of £25. They lost by 12 runs.

Employment as a professional coach

At the beginning of the 1855 season, H H was employed as a professional coach at Oxford University. He featured in a team of eleven professional players, selected from the 25 engaged by the University club at Oxford that season, in a match starting on 11 May against the Undergraduates of Oxford on the Magdalen College Ground. Later that month he played for Fuller Pilch and E Martin's XI against XXII of Christ Church College at Oxford.

From June H H was fully committed to the All England Eleven. He played in all of their 23 games that season, scoring an aggregate of 401 runs at an average of 11.14, with a highest score of 58. As a wicket-keeper he took 28 catches and made 14 stumpings.

The demise of William Clarke

In 1855 William Clarke was still in prodigious form with his slow underhand lobs and, at 56 years of age, he took a total of 91 wickets in five matches in June and early July. However, declining health and fitness saw him play his final game for the Eleven at Whitehaven in June 1856 when he took a wicket with the last ball he ever bowled. He umpired in the match beginning at Melton Mowbray on 10 July 1856, but this was to be his last appearance in any capacity on a cricket field as he died in Wandsworth, Surrey, on 25 August 1856.

In 189 matches for his All England Eleven William Clarke took 2,385 wickets, and in 302 innings he scored 1,339 runs at an average of 5.72.

GEORGE PARR.

From the Collection of Mr A. J. Gaston, Brighton.

George Parr (above) was elected Secretary of the All England Eleven and, at a meeting on 26 September 1856, a committee of management was formed, consisting of

Julius Caesar, Edgar Willsher, George Anderson, Alfred Clarke and H H to carry on the Eleven as previously.

Conclusion

The formation of an All England Eleven was a revolutionary concept which helped the spread of the game throughout the country. It gave earning potential to professional cricketers such as H H Stephenson and provided them with a platform from which they could further their careers.

[1] Wynne-Thomas, Peter, *Trent Bridge – A History of the Ground to commemorate the 150th Anniversary 1838-1988*, Nottinghamshire County Council, Nottingham, 1987, p.13
[2] *Frederick Lillywhite's Cricket Scores and Biographies of Celebrated Cricketers*, vol. III: 1841-1848, Frederick Lillywhite, London, 1863, p.461
[3] Caffyn, William, *Seventy-one not out: the reminiscences of William Caffyn*, William Blackwood & Sons, Edinburgh and London, 1899, p.24
[4] *Frederick Lillywhite's Cricket Scores and Biographies of Celebrated Cricketers from 1841 to 1848*, vol. IV: 1849-1854, Frederick Lillywhite, London, 1863, p.430
[5] Lillywhite, Frederick, *The Guide to Cricketers*, Eighth Edition, Frederick Lillywhite, London, 1855, p.54
[6] *M C C Cricket Scores and Biographies*, vol. V: 1855-1857, Longmans & Co., London, 1876, p.189
[7] Bailey, Philip; Thorn, Philip and Wynne-Thomas, Peter, *Who's Who of Cricketers*, Hamlyn, London, 1992, p.173
[8] Matthews, Bryan, *The Book of Rutland*, Barracuda Books Ltd., Buckingham, 1978, p.49
[9] Caffyn, William, *Seventy-one not out: the reminiscences of William Caffyn*, p.54
[10] *M C C Cricket Scores and Biographies*, vol. VI: 1858-1860, Longmans & Co., London, 1876, p.45
[11] Lillywhite, Frederick, *The Guide to Cricketers*, Eighth Edition, p.55
[12] Major, John, *More than a Game*, HarperCollins Publishers, London, 2007, p.155

4. THE YEAR OF THE HAT-TRICKS

This chapter surveys the years of Surrey's ascendancy and describes further landmarks in H H Stephenson's early career.

Prosperity of the Surrey Club

When William Burrup took over the position of secretary at Surrey in 1855, membership stood at around 230. After just a few years it soon approached 1,000 so that the income had likewise quadrupled to about £2,000 per year. Under his guidance it became the custom of the Surrey Club to present every amateur who scored 50 runs in one innings with a bat, whilst every professional who achieved this was given a sovereign, known as 'talent money'. Apparently William Burrup always made the presentation himself at the steps of the pavilion and delivered a speech.[1]

This growing prosperity off the field was matched by a string of excellent playing results in the four years from 1856 until 1859. During this time Surrey played 22 first-class matches and won 19 of them, with only two defeats. The highlight was undoubtedly the defeat of England by an innings and 28 runs at Kennington Oval in July 1858. An innings of 102 by William Caffyn was the backbone of the Surrey total, whilst H H excelled with the ball, returning figures of 22.1-9-34-6 in the first innings and 37-14-61-6 in the second.

This particular result was celebrated at Kennington Oval with a special plaque. All the players were given a sovereign, with an extra collection of £13 for William Caffyn. Prize bats went to Messrs. Lane, Miller and Burbidge. At a dinner after the match H H, on behalf of the team, presented the secretary, William Burrup, with a clay pipe as thanks for his invaluable contributions to the development of the Surrey Club.[2]

Outstanding bowling performances

As a wicket-taker, H H was most successful in 1858. Playing in 14 non first-class matches for the All England Eleven, he achieved figures for the season of 438.2-?-521-95 at an average of 5.48, whilst in 13 first-class matches he claimed 75 wickets at an average of 13.20.

In August 1858 H H played in the Married v Single first-class match at Kennington Oval, and William Caffyn heaped praise on the Single bowlers in the second innings: 'I never saw a bit of better bowling than that of Wisden and Stephenson neither of whom sent down a single loose ball.'[3]

H H's bowling was inspirational throughout the season. Playing for England against Kent at Lord's in July, he dismissed the last three batsmen in three balls. Kent had been strengthened by the inclusion of George Parr and John Jackson of Nottinghamshire and William Caffyn of Surrey, but they were rather outplayed, and George Parr was dismissed in both innings by H H.

A month later, playing for England against Eighteen Veterans at Kennington Oval, H H achieved the same feat: 'Stephenson with the last ball of an over bowled out Napper, and with the first two of his next he bowled out Box and Mynn.'[4]

At the end of August H H was once again in devastating form for the All England Eleven. In the fixture at Truro against XXII of East Cornwall he had the impressive match figures of 56.2-?-36-14. The following day, 2 September, the Eleven began a match at Plymouth against XXII of East Cornwall and South Devonshire but this three-day game had to be abandoned after just two hours because of rain. H H managed to take all five wickets which fell in that time, so he made the journey north to Sheffield in good form.

Making history in Sheffield

The match between the All England Eleven and XXII of Hallam and Staveley was eagerly awaited, as the Eleven had not played in Sheffield for several years. With good weather large crowds were attracted to the ground over the three days. In their very detailed coverage of the match, the local newspaper aptly summarised the numerical disadvantage which confronted the Eleven and led to their defeat by one wicket:

'The play of the eleven was in every respect excellent. As a fast bowler, Jackson is, probably, unequalled in the country...At the stumps, H H Stephenson could hardly be surpassed, and when he took the ball in the second inning used it most effectually. The fielding of the eleven, if we except one or two slips, to which the best hands are liable, was almost faultless. The batting of the eleven was, on the whole, equal to their fielding, that of Anderson, Daft, and Parr being particularly admired...All, however,...experienced, in its fullest extent, the disadvantage of contending against so numerous a field as twenty-two, for the provincials were so thick on the ground and fielded so ably, that the chances of scoring, except by an occasional drive right over the field, were indeed small.'[5]

The bowling feat of H H, which has taken its place in cricketing history, was described in the following way in the *Sheffield and Rotherham Independent* of 11 September 1858:

Young (a left handed batter) now joined E. Stephenson, who held his bat so obstinately that two other changes were resorted to—Jackson changing ends; H. H. Stephenson receiving the ball from Parr, and Davis going to the wicket In Jackson's second over after the change, Young made a fine cut for three. The third ball of H. H. Stephenson's second over took E. Stephenson's wicket, and he retired for a score of 21, won by extremely good playing. It was now more than half-past one, and the score was 52 for three wickets down. Before the dinner-bell rang at two, no less than four other wickets had fallen, the three first without adding at all to the score, and the last with only an addition of three. They were Young, Hawksworth, Hopkinson, and Champion. Hawksworth was caught from the third ball of Stephenson's fourth over; Hopkinson bowled by the next ball in the same over; and Champion was caught from the first ball of Stephenson's fifth over, three players being thus disposed of by three successive balls from the same hand. We understand that Stephenson was presented with a guinea for this extraordinary feat.

Financially this match was a great success for Mrs Heathcote, who had agreed to lend the ground and incur half the expenses on condition of receiving half the profits. The expenses amounted to £120, being £66 for the All England Eleven and the cost of the professional players on the opposing side, together with the costs of advertising. With an admission charge of 6d. and around 7,500 spectators attending during the three days, it left Mrs Heathcote and the Hallam and Staveley committees with a handsome profit. The full scorecard from the newspaper of that same date was as follows:

First innings.	ALL ENGLAND.		Second innings.	
F. P. Miller, Esq., c. Hawksworth, b Sherman	8	c. Sherman, b Tinley	0
Davis, c Stephenson, b Tinley	1	c Thorpe, b Sherman	1
R. Daft, Esq., b Sherman	20	c A. Waterfall, b Sherman	7
Diver, c Dawes, b Tinley	2	b Tinley	9
Geo. Parr, c W. Waterfall, b Tinley	13	b Tinley	13
Cæsar, b Tinley	0	b Tinley	16
Anderson, c Young, b Tinley	0	not out	28
A. Clarke, c Stephenson, b Tinley	6	s Stephenson, b Tinley	0
Jackson, c and b Sherman	3	run out	0
H. H. Stephenson, not out	1	c Madin, b Tinley	10
Gibson, c Lieut. Elmhirst, b Tinley	0	b Tinley	0
Bye 1, wide 3	4	Bye 1, wide 1	2
Total	**58**	**Total**	**107**

HALLAM AND STAVELEY.				
First Innings.		Second Innings.	
H. Creswick, b Gibson	7	b Stephenson	1
Keeton, run out, b Jackson	8	c Clarke, b Parr	14
J. Hawksworth, c Cæsar, b Jackson	0	c Jackson, b Stephen.	0
Champion, c Anderson, b do.	3	c Daft, b Stephenson	2
Dawes, b Jackson	1	c. Jackson, b do.	0
Hopkinson, b Jackson	2	b Stephenson	0
E. Stephenson, c Diver b Gibson	5	b Stephenson	21
Col. Elmhirst, b Jackson	0	run out	0
J. Thorpe, st Stephenson, b Gibson	5	c. Parr, b Stephenson	0
Wildgoose, b Jackson	0	b Jackson	10
A. Waterfall, c Parr, b do.	0	b Jackson	16
Young, c Anderson, b Gibson	5	run out	6
W. Waterfall, run out	2	b Jackson	2
H. Elmhirst, Esq., b Jackson	10	b Jackson	1
W. Horsley, b Jackson	0	not out	0
T. Sherman, c. Miller, Esq., b. Jackson	2	b. Jackson	3
Tinley, run out	0	b. Stephenson	2
Berresford, st. Stephenson, b. Gibson	5	not out	1
Lieut. Perry, b. Jackson	5	c. Gibson, b. Jackson	0
M. Kenyon run out	1	b. Stephenson	0
H. Madin not out	1	c. Davis, b. Gibson	6
C. Thornhill, l. b. w., b. Jackson	0	b. Stephenson	0
Leg bye	1	b. 5; l. b. 3, n. b. 1	9
Total	**68**	**Total**	**103**

ANALYSIS OF THE BOWLING.

HALLAM BOWLERS.—ENGLAND FIRST INNINGS.

	Runs from bat.	Wides.	Ttl.	Byes.	Ovrs.	Mdn.	bowld.	Ct. & st.
T. Sherman.	25	3	28	1	27	10	1	2
F. Tinley	29	0	29	0	27¼	9	1	6

HALLAM BOWLERS.—ENGLAND SECOND INNINGS.

| T. Sherman | 65 | 1 | 66 | 1 | 38¼ | 18 | 0 | 2 |
| F. Tinley | 40 | 0 | 40 | 0 | 36 | 12 | 7 | 3 |

ENGLAND BOWLERS.—HALLAM FIRST INNINGS.

| J. Jackson | 23 | 0 | 23 | 1 | 37 | 26 | 8 | 4 |
| R. Gibson | 39 | 0 | 39 | 0 | 36 | 16 | 1 | 4 |

ENGLAND BOWLERS.—HALLAM SECOND INNINGS.

J. Jackson	35	0	35	5	48	29	5	0
R. Gibson	18	0	18	3	14	8	0	1
G. Parr	12	0	12	0	6	1	0	1
Stephenson	29	1	30	0	26	10	8	5

Runs obtained at the fall of each Wicket:—

England.

	1	2	3	4	5	6	7	8	9	10
First Innings	2	15	21	45	48	48	48	55	58	58
Second Innings	1	10	27	88	39	41	68	88	97	107

Hallam and Staveley, First Innings.

1	2	3	4	5	6	7	8	9	10	11	12	13	14	15	16	17	18	19	20	21
12	12	16	18	20	21	21	31	31	39	36	37	39	39	41	45	52	60	62	63	68

Hallam and Staveley, Second Innings.

1	2	3	4	5	6	7	8	9	10	11	12	13	14	15	16	17	18	19	20
17	59	59	59	59	59	55	56	60	61	65	71	74	86	90	99	94	102	103	103

The mystique of the 'hat-trick'

It is widely acknowledged by historians of the game that the first recorded instance of a hat-trick – taking three wickets with three consecutive balls – was achieved by H H Stephenson at the Hyde Park Ground in Sheffield in September 1858, as recorded in the *Sheffield and Rotherham Independent* of 11 September 1858. It may be that a collection was taken at the ground in a hat, or that a hat was bought for him from the proceeds of the collection. Whatever the case, no written evidence seems to exist. We are left to assume that H H was awarded a hat in addition to the sovereign. Equally confounding is the fact that he had already achieved the same feat on two occasions earlier that season, so why were they overlooked? One explanation may be the following:

'Mr G B Buckley, writing on this subject in *The Cricketer* of St Swithun's Day, 1939, suggested that the Lord's and Oval hat-tricks may have been considered less meritorious (the victims being lower in the batting-order), or alternatively that the award took some other form.'[6]

It is known that in the 18th century David Harris of the Hambledon Cricket Club received a hat for an outstanding bowling performance,[7] so a precedent had already been set for rewarding a remarkable feat in the game. In later days a county cap was awarded to recognise such performances.

The feat of dismissing three batsmen in three balls had also been achieved in first-class matches by:

Alfred Mynn – **Fast Bowlers** v Slow Bowlers at Lord's, 1841

William Clarke – Kent v **England** at Canterbury, 1844

W J Hammersley – Surrey v **M C C** at Kennington Oval, 1848

James Dean – **England** v Nottinghamshire at Lord's, 1853

G H B Gilbert – Victoria v **New South Wales** at Melbourne, 1857-58[8]

Conclusion

The 1858 season confirmed the status of H H Stephenson as one of the leading cricketers of the day. With his hat-trick at the Hyde Park Ground in Sheffield, he wrote a piece of cricketing history and ensured himself a place forever in the sporting record books.

[1] Lemmon, David, *The Official History of Surrey County Cricket Club*, Christopher Helm, London, 1989, p.24
[2] Alverstone, Lord and Alcock, C W, *Surrey Cricket – its history and associations*, Longmans, Green and Co., London, 1902, p.152
[3] Caffyn, William, *Seventy-one not out: the reminiscences of William Caffyn*, William Blackwood & Sons, Edinburgh and London, 1899, p.132
[4] *M C C Cricket Scores and Biographies*, vol.VI: 1858-1860, Longmans & Co., London, 1876, p.119
[5] *Sheffield and Rotherham Independent*, 11 September 1858
[6] Martineau, G D, 'A Hat-Trick Centenary?' in *The Cricketer*: Spring Annual, London, 1958, p.52
[7] Major, John, *More than a Game*, HarperCollins*Publishers*, London, 2007, p.92
[8] Frindall, Bill, ed. *The Wisden Book of Cricket Records*, Queen Anne Press, 1986, pp.254-9

5. CRICKETING PIONEERS

A brief glimpse at H H Stephenson's family life and highlights of the 1859 season lead into an account of cricket's first ever overseas touring team.

Family matters

During the early part of the 1850s H H's mother, Mrs Catherine Stephenson, continued to live at Arbrook Common, Esher, with her house servant, Mary Ann Brittle. Her finances were limited, but she maintained an interest in her son's cricketing career. In an undated letter to 'My dear Boy' she acknowledges receipt of money from her son, continuing: 'I long to know how you got on at Brighton. I went to Esher yesterday for a look at Harry's paper and saw Miller out for 9, Julie not out 19, somebody else not out 17, against 122.'[1] This clearly refers to the Sussex v Surrey match which started on the Royal Brunswick Ground, Hove, on 20 June 1856 and resulted in victory for Surrey by nine wickets in two days.

On 27 October 1858 H H married Jemima Edmead in the Parish Church of St George the Martyr in Southwark, where one of the witnesses was Edgar Willsher, the Kent and All England Eleven fast bowler. Sadly, however, their happiness was short-lived. Jemima had been suffering from a kidney disease for three years and died at Thames Ditton on 13 March 1859, less than six months after the wedding, having been in a coma for eight days.

At about this time the family moved into terraced properties along the main Portsmouth Road, in the parish of Thames Ditton. H H lived at 3, Myrtle Cottages, whilst his mother and her house servant occupied no.1.

A varied programme of matches

Together with Iddison, Tinley, Willsher and Wright, H H was engaged as a bowler to the Manchester Broughton Club during the 1859 season, but this commitment did not prevent him from playing elsewhere in first-class matches.

In an interview H H modestly recalled the following incident from these days:

'I remember once going from Cambridge to Esher with Caffyn, who was going to stay there with me. We had each made over a hundred. The railway carriage was full of people who had seen the match, and they began to talk about it, but did not know us. We were tired and did not join in the conversation, although it was difficult not to do so, when a man suddenly exclaimed, "By Jove, I should like to be able to play like those men. Oh, if only I could manage to rub up against them, perhaps some of their cleverness would come to me!"'[2]

On this occasion, towards the end of May, H H and William Caffyn had been playing for Surrey against 16 Undergraduates of Cambridge on F P Fenner's Ground, but H H rather exaggerated his own contribution with the bat! Caffyn did score 157 in the Surrey innings but H H was dismissed for 35 before claiming match figures of 10-115 with the ball.

H H Stephenson and William Caffyn
Reproduced by kind permission of
Surrey C C C Archive

He further enhanced his reputation as a bowler at Sleaford that season with an analysis of 35-?-24-11 when the All England Eleven dismissed XXII of Sleaford for a meagre total of 52 in their first innings. In their next match together for Surrey at Kennington Oval, H H and William Caffyn bowled unchanged throughout both innings of the Marylebone Cricket Club, H H claiming five wickets and Caffyn twelve wickets, with three batsmen run out.

Two matches at Kennington Oval in July were of particular interest that season. In their only match of the season Nottinghamshire defeated Surrey by eight wickets, with George Parr hitting 130 runs. This represented his highest score in first-class cricket and it was the first century ever made for Nottinghamshire.[3]

He then followed this by scoring 108 runs in England's second innings. It was a unique all-round performance. These were the only two defeats inflicted on Surrey that summer.

Setting sail for Canada

In the middle of August Mr Wilder, President of the Cricketers' Fund, and Mr Pickering of the Montreal Club had reached an agreement for a cricket tour of North America by twelve players led by George Parr and John Wisden. The touring party consisted of George Parr (captain), James Grundy and John Jackson of Nottinghamshire; Julius Caesar, William Caffyn, H H Stephenson and Thomas Lockyer of Surrey; John Lillywhite and John Wisden of Sussex and Robert Carpenter, Alfred Diver and Tom Hayward

Carpenter. Caffyn. Lockyer. Wisden. Stephenson. G. Parr. Grundy. Cæsar. Hayward. Jackson.
Diver.   John Lillywhite.

FIRST AMERICAN TEAM.

Photographed on board ship at Liverpool, Sept. 7, 1859.

Later that month, when England defeated Surrey by 392 runs, V E Walker of Middlesex, who was captain of the England side, captured all ten Surrey wickets in their first innings for an analysis of 43-17-74-10.

of Cambridgeshire. The players were to receive £50 each with all expenses paid, and Fred Lillywhite, with his printing press and tent, acted as the official reporter of the matches.

The party set sail from Liverpool on 7 September on the *S S Nova Scotian* and for much of the voyage had to endure rough seas:

'Caffyn and Stephenson here attempted the task of going below, when an alarming pitch at the moment caused them both to be precipitated to the bottom of the steps, and nothing more was seen of them for two days and a half.'[4]

The ship was blown off course and was well behind schedule. When conditions were favourable the players enjoyed games of shuffle-board in the day whilst games of whist and the occasional concert occupied their evenings. After a delightful journey down the St Lawrence River they finally reached Quebec on 22 September and then travelled by train to Montreal.

between six of the All England Eleven and six of the United All England Eleven, with the addition of five Canadians on each side. The All England Eleven was represented by Parr, Stephenson, Caesar, Haywood, Diver and Jackson, but they lost the match by an innings and 54 runs.

The players remained in Montreal until Saturday 1 October when they undertook the 450-mile journey to New York, which involved several changes from one railway company to another before they transferred to a river-boat at Albany for the over-night journey to New York. Out of curiosity large crowds gathered at the St George's Club at Hoboken to watch the English players, who won the match by an innings and 64 runs, with Caffyn claiming 16 wickets in the home side's second innings. Once again a

'Four Horse Bus', reproduced from Lillywhite's book (see note 4)

Enthusiastic receptions

Wherever the party went, they were warmly welcomed, and at the start of their first match two days later against XXII of Lower Canada around 3,000 spectators had gathered at the ground. That Saturday evening a splendid banquet was organised for the players at the St Lawrence Hotel. In the match George Parr took sixteen wickets and the visitors won by eight wickets. A further game was played in Montreal

supplementary match was played, this time between H H Stephenson's XI and Lockyer's XI, with five gentlemen each from the United States. A dinner at Astor House was accompanied by the usual speeches, toasts and national anthems.[5]

On Saturday 8 October the party left by train for Philadelphia, but because of the wet weather and then the local elections no play was possible until the Wednesday. That day it was enthusiastically reported that 'nothing could present a more delightful aspect than the collection together of so large a number of American ladies, seated by themselves, tastefully dressed in every variety of modern costume, and forming, by the combination of the colours of their dresses and the attractiveness of their countenances, one of the most delightful pictures that the eye of man could rest upon.'[6] The standard of play of the home side was better than that of their previous opponents, although the visitors were victorious by seven wickets. They were regally entertained by members of the club and the proprietors of the Girard House Hotel. As usual, a further match was played, this time between players representing the North and South of England, assisted by six Americans on each side, and this game was won comfortably by the North by 61 runs.

On Saturday 15 October, the party travelled by train to Buffalo and then to Niagara Falls by 'Four Horse Bus' (see previous page) before reaching Hamilton for their next game against XXII of Upper Canada. In this match H H made his most significant contribution of the tour with bowling figures of 30-19-19-7 in the opposition's first innings. The visitors won by ten wickets.

A further game against XXII of the United States and Canada had been arranged at Rochester, just over 200 miles away. Cold weather on the Friday followed by snow the following day restricted play, but this did not deter the team from returning to Niagara on the Sunday to admire the Falls again, this time from the Canadian side. The match eventually ended in victory by an innings and 68 runs for the tourists, who thus remained undefeated on the tour.[7]

Immediately after this game the players headed back to Montreal and then on to Quebec where they boarded the *S S North Briton* for the voyage home on 29 October. The weather was even worse than they had experienced on the outward journey and one of the sailors died as the result of an accident. They reached Liverpool on Friday 11 November, having covered 7,500 miles in just over two months during the tour.

A dinner took place in Godalming, Surrey, on 8 December to celebrate the return of the southern players and to congratulate them on their achievements; it was attended by the Surrey and Sussex members of the touring party.

Conclusion

The death of H H's wife Jemima was a sad prelude to the 1859 cricketing season. Nevertheless, with his usual enthusiasm and determination, he embarked upon the new season which culminated in an invitation to tour North America. Despite the physical discomforts of their adventurous journey, all members of this first touring party could look back with great satisfaction at their efforts on the field of play and the generous hospitality afforded by their hosts.

[1] Letter from Mrs Catherine Stephenson to H H, in the collection of John Oakley, undated
[2] *The Cricket Field*, 1 June 1895, p.142
[3] Wynne-Thomas, Peter, *George Parr*, Famous Cricketers Series: No.20, Association of Cricket Statisticians and Historians, West Bridgford, 1993, p.19
[4] Lillywhite, Frederick, *The English Cricketers' Trip to Canada and the United States in 1859*, with an introduction by Robin Marlar, World's Work Ltd., Tadworth, 1980, p.5
[5] *ibid.*, p.36
[6] *ibid.*, p.40
[7] *ibid.*, p.50

6. AN AUSTRALIAN ADVENTURE

The popularity of H H Stephenson led to his captaining the first English team to tour Australia. This chapter looks at events leading to the team's departure and the matches that they played there.

A lively personality

Standing 6ft. tall, H H had a powerful physical presence in public, and he was often seen wearing a black frock-coat. George Parr therefore gave him the nickname 'Spurgeon', from the English popular Baptist preacher Charles Haddon Spurgeon (1834-92).[1]

He could also enjoy lighter and more frivolous moments with his colleagues in the Surrey dressing-room and he often played up to the skylarking antics of Julius Caesar: 'There was one particular tune that whenever he used to whistle old Julius Caesar would at once start up and walk round and round the room, and the quicker Stephenson whistled the faster went Julius.'[2]

Wicket-keeping

Hitherto H H had acquired a reputation as a formidable break-back bowler, and in the Surrey v North of England game at Kennington Oval in July 1861 'H H Stephenson sent Hayward a shooter that pitched a foot to the off and shot across taking the leg stump. 'Twas a wonderful ball.'[3] To some extent, however, this talent deserted him after a few years when he seemed to 'lose his command over the pitch of the ball…After a while he fell off in his bowling, which was chiefly owing to his having to do so much of it, and he in a manner lost the use of his fingers somewhat.'[4]

As his bowling suffered, so his wicket-keeping prospered. He began to keep wicket on a regular basis for the All England Eleven when Tom Lockyer, the Surrey wicket-keeper, moved over to play for the United All England Eleven. Even so, his position as wicket-keeper did not necessarily preclude him from bowling at some stage in a game.

William Caffyn considered him a first-class keeper who '…stood up to the wicket in the modern manner.'[5]

In September 1860 the All England Eleven paid their first visit to Ireland, playing XXII of Ireland in Dublin and then XXII of the North of Ireland in Belfast, and H H kept wicket in these games.

Assembling a touring team

Encouraged by the success of the overseas tour to North America, Spiers and Pond, a Melbourne catering firm, mindful of the growing popularity of cricket in their country, tried to attract a team of leading English players to Australia. They sent their agent, W B Mallam, to England in August 1861, offering £150 per player plus first-class travel and expenses. The offer was turned down by George Parr, captain of the touring team to North America, as he considered the money insufficient, but support came from William Burrup, Surrey's honorary secretary, who recruited six of his Surrey players.

Several prominent cricketers of the time such as Wisden, Julius Caesar and Richard Daft also rejected the offer, so the side that was eventually chosen in late September did not represent the strongest team that might have been raised. H H was confirmed as the captain of a touring party that comprised William Caffyn, William Mortlock, George Griffith, William Mudie and Tom Sewell Jun., all of Surrey; Roger Iddison and Ned Stephenson of Yorkshire; Tom Hearne and Charles Lawrence of Middlesex; George Wells of Sussex and George Bennett of Kent. Membership of these early touring sides was by the invitation of the organisers or sponsors who considered them as profit-making ventures.

George Wells and his wife had left for Australia earlier but the other eleven players travelled on the *S S Great Britain*

Mortlock. Mudie. Bennett. Lawrence. H. H. Stephenson. Caffyn. Griffith. Hearne. Iddison. Sewell. E. Stephenson.

Mr W. B. Mallam.

FIRST ENGLAND ELEVEN IN AUSTRALIA.

Taken just previous to their departure for Australia, October 1861.

from Liverpool on 20 October 1861. After an uneventful voyage they disembarked on Christmas Eve and travelled by coach into Melbourne for a tumultuous welcome.[6]

The opening matches

The first game was played on the Richmond cricket ground in Melbourne, beginning on New Year's Day. Around 25,000 spectators and glorious sunshine greeted the players at the start of the game against XVIII of Victoria, H H having persuaded the organising committee to field only 18, rather than 22, of Victoria. On the day the players wore hat-bands and sashes of different colours so that the spectators could recognise them, and the colours were printed on the scorecards. Each day's play was punctuated by long luncheon breaks with banquets for large numbers of guests. These were followed by the usual toasts and speeches, and H H soon acquired a reputation as a lively public speaker. The tourists amassed a total of 305 in their only innings and they won the match by an innings and 96 runs. Caffyn's 79 was the highest individual score made by a member of the Eleven on this tour. With an admission charge of half-a-crown Spiers and Pond had covered all the costs of the tour by the

end of the third day, so they were exceedingly happy.[7]

William Hammersley, in *The Herald*, described this first game as a 'test match'. In his *Victorian Cricketers' Guide* for that season, he subsequently wrote that 'of the 13 matches played on the tour only five could be called test matches – the three played at Melbourne and the two played at Sydney.'[8] The second match involved a 200-mile journey over rough and bumpy roads by stagecoach to Beechworth where the XXII of the Ovens District were heavily defeated by an innings and 191 runs. The visitors then returned to Melbourne for a match against XXII of Victoria and New South Wales. With the home side putting up a good fight, the tourists were probably relieved to emerge with a draw in front of more large crowds. In the second innings Griffith took over as wicket-keeper and H H returned the excellent bowling figures of 7-23.

The party travelled by train to Geelong for their match against XXII of Geelong and the Western District, with the last stretch completed in a Cobb & Co. stagecoach driven by the legendary Australian coach driver Edward Devine.[9] H H's men won the game easily by nine wickets, mainly because of the excellent bowling of Sewell who claimed 15 wickets in the home side's second innings.[10]

More sea journeys

The voyage to Sydney took almost three days. Huge crowds lined the quay on the team's arrival, just as they had done some weeks previously in Melbourne. A large crowd gathered each day on the Outer Domain where the erection of stands and a charge for admission were the cause of much local controversy. Sewell and Griffith bowled superbly once again to avoid possible embarrassment against the XXII of New South Wales, and the visitors won by 49 runs. Sir Stuart Young, the Colonial Governor, and his entourage were present on each day. After the match a grand banquet was organised for the tourists, when the Governor presented H H with a diamond and sapphire ring (later bequeathed to his daughter Frances).

A difficult coach journey across the Blue Mountains took them to Bathurst where a noisy welcome awaited them. The match against XXII of Bathurst was abandoned because of rain before a gala dinner gave rise to the customary compliments from H H, who was later presented with a gold chain.[11]

Returning by coach to Sydney, the tourists found that the boat carrying the players from Victoria had been delayed by rough seas. They therefore agreed to entertain the spectators with a scratch match in which H H managed to score a few runs. In the match against XXII of New South Wales and Victoria on the Outer Domain, the tourists were dismissed cheaply for 60 and 75, losing their first match by twelve wickets. This first victory by a colonial side was hailed as a significant moment in Australian cricket history.[12]

William Caffyn reflected on the endless round of receptions to which the team had already been treated during their tour: 'We once more had high jinks at Sydney during our second stay there.

Scarcely a day passed without our being entertained to champagne breakfasts, luncheons and dinners. A performance at the Victorian theatre was given for our benefit, the house being simply packed. Between the pieces H H Stephenson read out a farewell address.'[13]

From Sydney the tourists sailed back to Melbourne and then across the Bass Strait before landing at Launceston, from where they continued by coach on the 150-mile journey to Hobart. A lively welcome came from the band of the rifle corps who escorted them to their hotel.

The XXII of Tasmania comprised players from both the Launceston and Hobart areas. A win by four wickets coincided with a good all-round performance by H H. He claimed three stumpings before taking the vital wicket of T Whitesides, the only player to score a half century against the tourists on the tour. H H then guided his side to victory with 23 not out. As the match finished early on the third day, an exhibition match was played between two teams captained by E Stephenson and H H, followed by a dinner which brought to an end their short stay in Tasmania.[14]

The final stage of the tour

On their return to Melbourne the tourists confronted each other in a match between The World XI and a Surrey XI. It was classified as a first-class match and so it appears in H H's career statistics in Appendix 2 (cf. p.57). The six Surrey players were joined by five local players who claimed to have links with the county, forming the Surrey XI. The World XI consisted of the other members of the touring party together with another five locals. Thanks to an outstanding all-round performance by Bennett, who scored 72 runs and then took 7-30 and 7-85 with his slow bowling, the World XI won by six wickets.

Before the start of this match news finally reached Melbourne of the sudden death on 14 December 1861 of Prince

Albert, the occasion for great sadness and mourning.[15]

The tourists then met with varied success in three fixtures played in the gold-mining areas of north-western Victoria. A drawn game against XXII of Ballarat was followed by an innings victory at Bendigo where H H made 47, his highest score of the tour, and Bennett took 23 wickets in the match. The pitch at Castlemaine was in a poor condition and this may have contributed to defeat for the tourists by three wickets.

They took the coach to Melbourne for the last game which was organised by Spiers and Pond for the sole benefit of the All England Eleven. It remained unfinished, the visitors requiring just eleven runs to win with three wickets standing.

The tour ended on the happiest of notes. At the close of play the tourists planted elm saplings around the sides of the Melbourne ground. There was then a series of moving farewells and gifts, with H H expressing his pride in the achievements of his players. Spiers and Pond offered the players a further £1,200 to stay in Australia for another month, but they turned down this offer because of their commitments back in England. However, Charles Lawrence had accepted a position as coach of the Albert Club in Sydney at a salary of £300 per year, so he stayed behind in Australia.[16]

The return journey was partly by sea on the *R M S Northam* with the final stage overland, so that the team arrived back in England on 12 May 1862.

Conclusion

Although it was not a truly representative national team, the English players were hailed as professional ambassadors for the game, and their general conduct in Australia won them many friends and attracted large crowds. H H Stephenson's contribution to the success of the tour was significant. As a player he kept wicket immaculately and

made some useful contributions as a batsman in the later matches. Carrying out the roles of spokesman and diplomat impeccably, he commanded respect with inspiring leadership which helped the tour to run so smoothly.

[1] Caffyn, William, *Seventy-one not out: the reminiscences of William Caffyn*, William Blackwood & Sons, Edinburgh and London, 1899, p.91
[2] Daft, Richard, *Kings of Cricket: anecdotes and reminiscences from 1858 to 1892*, Tillotson & Son, Bolton, 1893, p.75
[3] *Baily's Magazine of Sports and Pastimes*, A H Baily & Co., London, 1861
[4] Caffyn, William, *Seventy-one not out: the reminiscences of William Caffyn*, p.91
[5] *ibid.*, p.91
[6] Frith, David, *The Trailblazers: The First English Cricket Tour of Australia 1861-62*, Boundary Books, Goostrey, 1999, pp.57-9
[7] Moyes, A G, *Australian Cricket: a History*, Angus & Robertson Ltd., Sydney and Melbourne, 1959, pp.130-2
[8] Harte, Chris, *A History of Australian Cricket*, Andre Deutsch Ltd., London, 1993, p.67
[9] Austin, K A, 'Devine, Edward (1833-1908)' in *Australian Dictionary of Biography*, 1972, Online Edition
[10] *Baily's Magazine of Sports and Pastimes*, 1862, p.260
[11] Frith, David, *The Trailblazers: The First English Cricket Tour of Australia 1861-62*, p.127
[12] *ibid.*, p.130
[13] Caffyn, William, *Seventy-one not out: the reminiscences of William Caffyn*, p.180
[14] Harte, Chris, *A History of Australian Cricket*, p.69
[15] Frith, David, *The Trailblazers: The First English Cricket Tour of Australia 1861-62*, p.139
[16] Harte, Chris, *A History of Australian Cricket*, p.70

7. A DECADE OF CHANGE

The changing face of cricket, with its jealousies and regional tensions, gave rise to divisions within the game and ultimately hastened the demise of the travelling Elevens. H H Stephenson happily accepted the opportunity to represent a number of professional sides.

Repercussions from the tour to Australia

Although the tour had been a great success, it had engendered ill-feeling among certain professionals, who felt that the inclusion of six Surrey players and a further four from the counties of Kent, Middlesex and Sussex showed an undue bias towards southern players. Equally other professionals were unhappy at the manner in which negotiations had been conducted. The appointment of H H as captain of the touring side also aroused a little jealousy. All this led to hostility towards Surrey.

Another possible reason for this ill-feeling was that the county was comparatively rich and paid its professionals better than most counties. In addition, most of the Surrey team were professionals who had collectively negotiated favourable pay and conditions of work.[1]

Divisions within the game

The Gentlemen v Players fixture was played for the first time at Lord's in 1806 but no further match took place until 1819. After this date matches were held almost every year, and it was considered to be 'the most time-honoured of all representative matches'.[2] The Gentlemen, or amateurs, were men of leisure who played cricket for pleasure, whereas the Players, or paid professionals, were frequently from a more rustic or working-class background. It is therefore unusual to find the son of a surgeon such as H H playing as a professional, but financial circumstances undoubtedly dictated this. To accentuate the class division 'amateurs changed in separate dressing rooms, entered the playing area through separate gates, and ate apart from the professionals.'[3] At that time the Players generally held the upper hand in the fixture. In the 14 matches in which H H played between 1857 and 1869 the Players were victorious on eleven occasions.

The formation of a United All England Eleven, led by John Wisden, arose in 1852 from a grievance by those southern professionals who felt that they were not receiving a proper financial reward from

LILLYWHITE'S PRINTING TENT.

Printed and Published on the Ground, BY AUTHORITY and under the Distinguished PATRONAGE of the MARYLEBONE CLUB, by Frederick Lillywhite, of 2, New Coventry Street, Leicester Square.

At LORD'S   The United All England Eleven agst The All England Eleven Monday, Tuesday, & Wednesday, June 1st 2nd & 3rd 1857.

United	First Innings		Second Innings	
T. Hunt	b Willsher	0	b Jackson	6
J. Dean	b Jackson	36	b Willsher	0
J. Grundy	b Bickley	9	c Jackson, b Tinley	27
W. Caffyn	b Jackson	38	c Jackson, b Willsher	4
J. Wisden	b Jackson	7	b Jackson	7
H. Wright	c Crossland, b Jackson	7	b Tinley	21
John Lillywhite	run out	11	c Stephenson, b Bickley	11
F. Bell	not out	10	b Willsher	33
T. Lockyer	b Willsher	5	b Willsher	4
W. Mortlock	l b w. b Jackson	2	b Willsher	7
W. Martingell	c Diver, b Jackson	4	not out	7
	b 11, l-b 5, w 1, n-b	17	b 10, l-b 1, w , n-b 2,	13
	Total	143	Total	140

All England	First Innings		Second Innings	
A. Diver	c Dean, b Wisden	0		
A. Crossland	b Caffyn	24	c Wisden, b Lillywhite	5
H. Stephenson	c & b Caffyn	51	b Lillywhite	5
G. Parr	not out	56	not out	19
J. Cæsar	b Caffyn	9	not out	0
R. C. Tinley	b Martingell	9	b Caffyn	23
G. Anderson	b Caffyn	0	run out	10
A. Clarke	run out	0	c Bell, b Caffyn	9
E. Willsher	b Caffyn	20		
J. Bickley	b Caffyn	8		
J. Jackson	b Caffyn	12		
	6, l-b 8, w 1, n-b 2,	17	b 4, l-b 2, w 1, n-b ,	7
Umpires Sewell & Barker	Total	206	Total	78

MATCHES TO COME:
Thursday, June 4, at Lord's ...Grand Military match, with Bands
Monday, June 8, at Lord's [Ascot week]...M C C and Ground against County of Kent
Thursday, June 11, at Lord's...No match fixed
Monday, June 15, at Lord's...M C C and Ground against County of Sussex
Thursday, June 18, at Lord's...No match fixed
Thursday, June 18, at Oxford...M C C and Ground against Undergraduates of Oxford.
Saturday, June 20, at Eton...M C C against present Etonians.
Monday, June 22, at Lord's...Sixteen Gentlemen of the University of Cambridge against United All England Eleven. Mr Dark's match
Wednesday, June 24, at Lord's...M C C against present Rugbeans
The Tenth Edition of LILLYWHITE'S GUIDE to CRICKETERS, Price ONE SHILLING may be had on the Ground. Published by F. Lillywhite & Wisden, 2, New Coventry Street, Leicester Square; & Piper & Co.   For other matches &c. turn over

William Clarke. Upon Clarke's death in 1856, hostilities between the two sides came to an end and, with George Parr now leading the All England Eleven, two matches were organised between the two Elevens at Lord's. H H's 51 runs for the All England Eleven in this first game represented his highest score in a first-class match in 1857. The profit of £158 from the game was donated to the Cricketers' Fund Benefit Society. Its aim was to give temporary financial support to the families of cricketers who could no longer play competitively.

H H played on 14 occasions in these matches between 1857 and 1864. After the match in 1863 H H was appointed to the committee of the Cricketers' Fund Benefit Society.[4]

Another representative fixture was that between the South of England and the North of England; the first matches took place in 1836, at both Lord's and Leicester. H H achieved selection for the South in 1854, in his first full season as a professional. Honours were evenly shared in the years from 1854 until 1866, H H playing in 20 of the fixtures during that time.

These three representative fixtures were the focus of public attention and were fully reported in the local and national press. However, they reflected and reinforced those social, economic and regional differences which were proving so divisive within the game.

Growing antagonism towards Surrey

Various incidents adversely affected fixtures involving Surrey. In the match between Surrey and England at Kennington Oval on 26 August 1862, Edgar Willsher, playing for the England side, was no-balled six times by the umpire John Lillywhite for bowling with his hand above his shoulder. This led to Willsher and his fellow professionals in the England side walking off the field. Play continued the following day with a different umpire. As a result of this incident George Parr and his supporters refused to play in the match between the North of England and

Surrey at the Broughton Club in Manchester in August 1863.

A further incident occurred during the match between Surrey and Nottinghamshire at Kennington Oval in July 1865 when the last Surrey batsman, Sewell, was given not out by the Surrey umpire despite being out of his crease. With H H eventually scoring 75 not out, Surrey went on to win the game by one wicket, to the great annoyance of the Nottinghamshire players and spectators. George Parr had already refused to play in the two matches against Surrey that year, and the two counties did not meet again until 1868.

The match between Yorkshire and Surrey in June 1865 at Bramall Lane was devalued when five crack Yorkshire professionals refused to play, giving Surrey an easy victory by ten wickets. The match was not played at all in 1866. A similar situation arose at Lord's in July 1866 when the crack northern players refused to play in the South of England v North of England fixture, so that a farcical match resulted in victory for the home side by an innings and 43 runs.

Overarm bowling

In the early years of cricket underarm bowling had been the fashion but, with batsmen gaining the upper hand, bowlers began experimenting with new methods and actions in order to achieve more speed and greater guile. With the bowler's arm now raised, the ball was being propelled from shoulder height in what became known as round-arm bowling. Such an action generated greater pace and its critics pointed out that it was dangerous for the batsmen who did not have protective clothing. It severely questioned Rule 10 of the Laws of Cricket, which defined fair bowling. The debate simmered for many years before round-arm bowling was finally accepted in 1835, allowing the bowler to raise his hand to shoulder height.[5]

Some 20 years later round-arm bowlers began raising their arm above shoulder height, but umpires accepted the situation even though it was illegal. The incident regarding Edgar Willsher, however, brought the matter to a head; in 1864 overarm bowling became legal. Law 10 was rewritten by the M C C so that a bowler's arm could be extended as high as he liked, provided he kept it straight and did not throw the ball.

The year 1864 was noteworthy in other ways. Firstly, it heralded the publication of *The Cricketer's Almanack* by John Wisden. Secondly, newspapers began publishing an unofficial table of results involving the counties of Cambridgeshire, Hampshire, Kent, Middlesex, Nottinghamshire, Surrey, Sussex and Yorkshire.

More regional divisions

The All England Eleven did not play any matches when George Parr was in Australia with the touring party, so Edgar Willsher and H H managed the 'English' Eleven who played three matches early in the 1864 season.

That same year renewed tensions between northern and southern cricketers led to the withdrawal of the southern cricketers – Julius Caesar, Edgar Willsher and H H – from the All England Eleven, whilst the other crack southern players resigned from the United All England Eleven. At a meeting held in London on 17 November 1864, the professionals from the south of England agreed to form the United South of England Eleven, their first match being at Dublin on 11 May 1865.[6] The All England Eleven was now composed entirely of northern players.

The Cricketer's Almanack,

FOR THE YEAR 1864,

BEING

Bissextile or Leap Year, and the 28th of the Reign of

HER MAJESTY QUEEN VICTORIA,

CONTAINING

The Laws of Cricket,

AS REVISED BY THE MARYLEBONE CLUB;

THE FIRST APPEARANCE AT LORD'S AND NUMBER OF RUNS OBTAINED BY

MANY CRICKETING CELEBRITIES;

SCORES OF 100 AND UPWARDS, FROM 1850 TO 1863;

EXTRAORDINARY MATCHES;

ALL THE MATCHES PLAYED BETWEEN

THE GENTLEMEN AND PLAYERS,

AND

The All England and United Elevens,

With full and accurate Scores taken from authentic sources;

TOGETHER WITH

The Dates of the University Rowing Matches,

THE WINNERS OF THE

DERBY, OAKS, AND ST. LEGER;

RULES OF

BOWLS, QUOITS, AND KNUR AND SPELL,

AND OTHER INTERESTING INFORMATION.

LONDON:

PUBLISHED AND SOLD BY JOHN WISDEN AND CO.,

AT THEIR

CRICKETING AND BRITISH SPORTS WAREHOUSE,

2, NEW COVENTRY STREET, HAYMARKET, W.

May be had of all respectable Booksellers in the United Kingdom, or forwarded free by the Publisher to any part of Great Britain for 13 Stamps.

1864. [One Shilling.

H H transferred his allegiance to this newly formed team, playing for them on an occasional basis from 1865. In July 1871 the team played at Uppingham in a match where W G Grace claimed 24 wickets but only scored one run in his two innings, as shown in this scorecard from Volume XII of *M C C Cricket Scores and Biographies*:

At UPPINGHAM, July 13, 14, and 15, 1871.

TWENTY-TWO OF UPPINGHAM, WITH J. C. SHAW.

T. Aris, l b w, b Silcock	0	— run out	8
W. H. Charlton, st Stephenson, b Mantle	3	— c Pooley, b Silcock	7
D. Royce, l b w, b W. G. Grace	38	— c W. G. Grace, b Silcock	2
H. R. Hunt, c Pooley, b W. G. Grace	28	— c Silcock, b W. G. Grace	6
S. Watson, c and b W. G. Grace	9	— c Street, b W. G. Grace	9
J. Furley, c R. Humphrey, b W. G. Grace	0	— c Mantle, b W. G. Grace	30
J. Letby, run out	0	— c W. G. Grace, b Silcock	5
J. Holdich, c Jupp, b W. G. Grace	2	— c Pooley, b W. G. Grace	5
N. Frisby, c Pooley, b Street	0	— b Silcock	13
W. Gay, c Stephenson, b W. G. Grace	29	— c Pooley, b W. G. Grace	6
C. J. Brown, c Holmes, b W. G. Grace	0	— c W. G. Grace, b Silcock	7
T. Whitsed, b Holmes	11	— st Pooley, b W. G. Grace	5
A. Beardsall, b W. G. Grace	4	— b W. G. Grace	1
A. W. Neilson, run out	3	— c W. G. Grace, b Silcock	3
W. Widdowson, b W. G. Grace	1	— c W. G. Grace, b Silcock	0
R. S. Thorpe, c R. Humphrey, b W. G. Grace	0	— c Stephenson, b W. G. Grace	0
H. Stuart, c Mantle, b W. G. Grace	0	— c W. G. Grace, b Silcock	4
J. C. Shaw, c Stephenson, b Holmes	0	— st Pooley, b W. G. Grace	0
M. Sneath, st Stephenson, b W. G. Grace	3	— c Holmes, b W. G. Grace	3
C. Tyler, c Pooley, b W. G. Grace	0	— not out	0
T. Bell, not out	4	— b W. G. Grace	1
W. Ingham, st Stephenson, b W. G. Grace	4	— b Silcock	4
Byes, &c.	4	Byes, &c.	6
	143		125

THE UNITED SOUTH OF ENGLAND ELEVEN.

W. G. Grace, Esq., c Charlton, b Watson	1	— run out	0
R. Humphrey, c Bell, b Shaw	26	— not out	55
G. F. Grace, Esq., run out	35	— c Royce, b Watson	7
H. Jupp, b Watson	2	— run out	31
E. Pooley, c Brown, b Shaw	0	— c Gay, b Shaw	4
T. Humphrey, c Watson, b Shaw	4	— not out	4
Frank Silcock, not out	9		
T. A. Mantle, c Beardsall, b Shaw	12		
H. Holmes, c substitute, b Shaw	2		
H. H. Stephenson, b Watson	1		
J. Street, c Neilson, b Shaw	2		
Byes, &c.	4	Byes, &c.	8
	98		109

Umpires—W. Brown and Julius Cæsar.

Unfinished.

Mr. W. G. Grace caught out 7, Stephenson stumped 3 and caught 3, and Pooley stumped 2 and caught 6.

Mr. W. G. Grace got 24 wickets, bowling down four only.

In addition to all this upheaval, The United North and South of England Eleven was formed in the autumn of 1866, but it played just two matches in 1867 and one in 1868 before coming to an end either through bad management or lack of support. This entirely new side had no pretensions to such a name as it was composed mainly of southern players who were relatively unknown in the world of cricket. However, the name served their purpose for arranging matches which would be profitable.

Conclusion

The schism between cricketers of the north and south of England became complete in 1864. The travelling Elevens had originally been very popular in the immediate locality of the towns where they played. As these Elevens became more numerous, however, so they became less important and steadily less attractive to the paying public, who were showing increasing interest in the county sides. Given his roots in Surrey, H H naturally aligned himself with the United South of England Eleven.

[1] Lemmon, David, *The Official History of Surrey County Cricket Club*, Christopher Helm, London, 1989, p.42
[2] Warner, Sir Pelham, *Gentlemen v Players 1806-1949*, George G Harrap & Co. Ltd., London, 1950, p.13
[3] Major, John, *More than a Game*, HarperCollins*Publishers*, London, 2007, p.268
[4] *M C C Cricket Scores and Biographies*, vol. VIII: 1863-1864, Longmans & Co., London, 1877, p.34
[5] Lewis, Tony, *Double Century: The Story of M C C and Cricket*, Hodder & Stoughton, London, 1987, p.76
[6] *M C C Cricket Scores and Biographies*, vol. IX: 1865-1866, Longmans & Co., London, 1877, p.12

8. THE DUC D'AUMALE AND WOOD NORTON

During the winter months H H Stephenson was still employed by the Duc d'Aumale, whose acquisition of the Wood Norton estate in Worcestershire now saw H H assume an even more prominent role than at Claremont. This chapter considers the involvement of both men in the local community and the county hunting scene.

The Wood Norton estate

Having entered the service of the Duc d'Aumale as a whipper-in and huntsman, H H was able to indulge his passion for field sports in the wider context when the Duc and his wife went to live at Wood Norton Hall, about two miles from Evesham. It was the property of Edward Holland who had been elected as Member of Parliament for Evesham. The Duc d'Aumale probably obtained the property under the terms of a lease or agreement of some kind.

The Duc d'Aumale

The estate comprised the village of Fladbury which, according to the 1861 Census, had a population of 411 inhabitants. To the east of Fladbury the River Avon was used extensively for commerce until the middle of

the century when the West Midland Railway began a regular service linking Evesham with Fladbury, Pershore and Worcester.

The Duchesse d'Aumale

After the turmoil of the early years of exile from France, the Duc and Duchesse came to Wood Norton in search of peace and tranquillity. With their interest in country pursuits they integrated themselves easily into the local community, showing concern for the well-being of neighbours and tenants on their estate.

Although the Duc and Duchesse did not reside permanently at Wood Norton, they wholeheartedly supported local initiatives and made donations to projects in the neighbourhood. The Duc donated £10 to a building fund for the use of the Evesham Institute[1] and £10 towards the restoration of Holy Cross Abbey Church at Pershore.[2] When a subscription list was opened for a new school in Fladbury in 1862, a large donation was made by the Duc d'Aumale. Contributions also came from other members of the gentry and the Bishop of Worcester. At a later date the Duc gave £5 for the Parish Church of North and Middle Littleton, together with £25 to the Restoration Fund for the Church of All Saints in Evesham.[3]

From *Kelly's Directory of Worcestershire, 1860*
Reproduced by kind permission of the Worcestershire Records Office

Elsewhere the Duchesse was listed as the principal Lady Patroness of the Evesham Institute on the occasion of The Grand Bazaar on 23 and 24 September 1862, whilst the Duc was an enthusiastic supporter of the Vale of Evesham Agricultural Association.

The Duc d'Aumale's Harriers

The first 'meet' of the Duc's pack of harriers at Norton received favourable coverage in *The Evesham Journal* of 23 March 1861:

The Duke d'Aumale's Harriers.

It will be very gratifying to the lovers of the old English sport of hunting, to hear that H. R. H. the Duke d'Aumale has established a Pack of Harriers, which he purposes hunting in our neighbourhood. On Tuesday last, the first "meet," which was almost of a private character, took place at Norton. There were two or three very good runs had, much to the delight of a considerable number of Equestrians and Pedestrians. Both on account of the spirit which it is likely to induce in the neighbourhood, and the congeniality to the English mind of the sport itself, the adoption of it, in so liberal a manner, by the distinguished Nobleman, who has become our neighbour, is hailed with much pleasure.

31

Further meets took place within the following week at Throckmorton, Pebworth and Cropthorne, and it was noted that 'the first-rate style in which everything is carried out must prove a great attraction to all lovers of the sport.'[4] After these meets the horses and hounds left by rail for Surrey.

The Duc's occasional residence at Wood Norton was the opportunity for him to extend generous hospitality to all his tenants and to the farmers in the neighbourhood over whose lands he had hunted during the season. On the morning of the meet proceedings began with breakfast for the invited guests, and when the meet was fixed for Mr Willetts of Bishampton Fields 'open housekeeping was the order of the day… where every comer was welcomed and hospitably entertained.'[5] On this occasion it was estimated that a crowd of around 500 were present to greet the royal party, which included the Prince de Joinville and the Duc de Chartres, and witness the 'uncarting' of a stag which had been brought up from the Royal Park at Richmond.

It was reported in *The Times* of 5 April 1865 that a royal stag hunt had provided a fitting end to the hunting season at Wood Norton. Members of the Worcestershire Hunt and other sporting gentlemen of the county had been invited to join his Royal Highness's famous pack of harriers for a meet fixed for the Northwick Arms, Bengeworth, a village to the south-east of Evesham.

In 1867 announcements of the meets of the Duc's Harriers appeared regularly in *The Evesham Journal*, and these took place each Tuesday and Saturday from 19 January until 19 March in both Worcestershire and Gloucestershire.

Serving the Duc d'Aumale as huntsman

The Duc d'Aumale led the life of a sporting country gentleman and was well respected by the local gentry, his tenants and servants. It must have been considered a great honour for H H to serve the Duc at this time, and he displayed unswerving loyalty towards him. Indeed, in September 1864, H H was prevented from playing in Julius Caesar's

testimonial match at Broadwater, near Godalming, 'having received the command of the Duc d'Aumale to be in attendance in Worcestershire.'[6]

As soon as the hunting or shooting season began, H H took up residence on the Craycombe estate in Fladbury. In the company of a housekeeper and general servant, H H lived close to Craycombe House at The Kennels, where he was responsible for the general welfare of the Duc's harriers. This involved feeding, walking and exercising the dogs, looking after any that were sick or lame and administering old remedies. Harriers were slightly smaller than foxhounds and were trained to hunt hares or foxes.[7]

Whilst working within an agreed budget H H was also responsible for arranging the meets. This involved liaison with farmers, selecting the harriers for the meet, drawing up a plan for the day and ensuring that all arrived at the meet on time at 11.00 or 11.30, when he would welcome all the followers:

> **The Duke D'Aumale's Harriers.**
> THE HUNTING SEASON.—His Royal Highness the Duke D'Aumale commenced the hunting season on Saturday last, the 4th inst. The meet took place at Cropthorne, at the residence of F. D. Holland, Esq. Soon after eleven o'clock H. H. Stephenson arrived with 13 couples of the right sort, and was met by a large field which included the Duke D'Aumale, the Prince De Conde, and most of the members of the Worcestershire Hunt. A hare was soon found near to the village and went away for the Gorse, where the hounds were taken off on account of a litter of cubs lying near that spot. Another hare was soon on foot and after about 20 minutes good hunting, she was pulled down by the merry little pack. A move was then made to the other side of the village, where puss was again found and made away for the railway—the hounds being hotly in pursuit of their game.

The Evesham Journal, 11 November 1865

Aided by whippers-in, he would use the weather conditions to his advantage, draw the cover to find a fox or hare and intervene whenever the scent evaporated. At the end of the meet they hacked back to The Kennels where the harriers were examined and any thorns were removed from their pads.

Royal visitors to Wood Norton

The Duc de Chartres

The visit of the Prince of Wales, the son of Queen Victoria, to Wood Norton received much coverage in *The Times* of 21 and 22 November 1867. The Prince came by special train, and a guard of honour awaited him at Evesham Station, where he was received by the Duc d'Aumale and presented to the Mayor. The short stay at Wood Norton was the opportunity for the Prince to engage in shooting on the Duc's estate and hunting with the Worcestershire Fox Hounds. Dinner parties were held each evening and invited guests included Prince Edward of Saxe-Weimar, the Earl and Countess of Dudley, the Duke of Beaufort,

The Prince de Condé

Mr H F Vernon, M P and Master of the Hunt, as well as the Duc de Chartres and the Duc d'Alençon.

A successful shoot in the coverts of Wood Norton yielded an impressive bag of 271 head, which included 229 pheasants, 2 woodcocks, 11 hares and 29 rabbits.

Royal mourning

Although several children were born of the Duc's marriage, some died in infancy. This misfortune continued when their eldest son, the Prince de Condé, died in Sydney, New South Wales, where he caught a typhus fever. The Wood Norton tenants sent the following message to the Duc d'Aumale:

'We hope that your Royal Highness will soon return to Wood Norton for although we feel that the return will be saddened by the associations which everything there will recall, we believe that in the retirement of that quiet home and in the interest which you take to all around it and in all that concerns your tenants and your neighbours you will find some mitigation of your sorrows.'[8]

Sadly the Duchesse found the loss of her eldest son difficult to bear. Notice of her failing health was soon followed by the news of her untimely death at Twickenham on Monday 6 December 1869 at 47 years of age. This was met with universal grief in the Evesham area where the Duc d'Aumale's family were held in such high esteem:

'The sympathy she always evinced in the pursuits of her noble Husband, her unaffected manners and courteous bearing, her kindness and affability, and her generosity to the poor, combined with her loyal devotion to her illustrious partner in the misfortunes of his House and the dignity in which those misfortunes have been borne, produced a deep feeling of admiration of the deceased Lady's character.'[9]

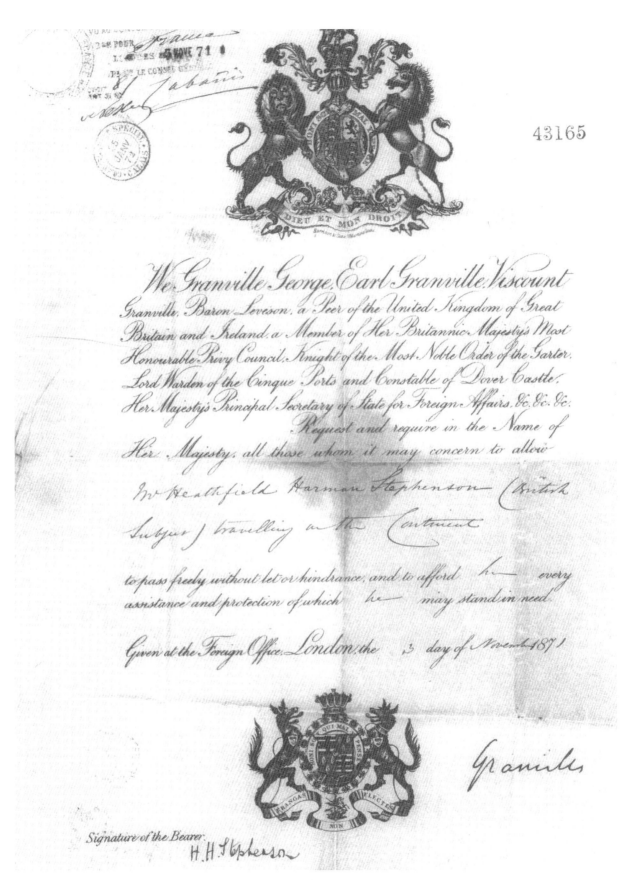

**Passport document issued to H H Stephenson to enable him to attend
the Royal Wedding at Chantilly (shown at just under half size)**

34

H H Stephenson's invitation to the wedding of Princesse Marguerite d'Orléans

A royal wedding

Serving the Duc as huntsman meant that H H became well acquainted with members of the French and English royal families, and on 15 January 1872 he attended the wedding of Princesse Marguerite d'Orléans, daughter of the Duc de Nemours and niece of the Duc d'Aumale. She married Prince Wladislaw Czartoryski, a Polish noble and political activist in exile, at Chantilly.

Conclusion

With his obliging and courteous manner and his skills at field sports, H H proved a great asset to the Duc d'Aumale at Wood Norton, becoming a popular member of the hunting fraternity around Evesham.

In turn the Duc and Duchesse d'Aumale endeared themselves to their neighbours by their generous hospitality and donations to local causes. The sudden deaths of their son and then of the Duchesse herself were deeply felt by everyone in the Evesham area.

H H's happy association with the Duc had seen him acquire a reputation as a fine huntsman and had brought him into contact with not only the local aristocracy but also the royal family. It had been a very exciting and fulfilling period of his life.

[1] *The Evesham Journal*, 18 May 1861
[2] *ibid.*, 21 December 1861
[3] *ibid.*, 18 March 1871
[4] *ibid.*, 30 March 1861
[5] *ibid.*, 28 March 1863
[6] *M C C Cricket Scores and Biographies*, vol. VI: 1858-1860, Longmans & Co., London, 1876, p.45
[7] Seaton, John, verbal communication, February 2009
[8] *The Evesham Journal*, 7 July 1866
[9] *ibid.*, 11 December 1869

9. A CRICKETING CRUSADE

Undaunted by the problems and tensions that occasionally afflicted the game in the 1860s, H H Stephenson accepted new challenges and reached significant milestones before his long association with the Surrey Club came to a happy conclusion.

A coaching appointment

Encouraged by the success of his leadership on the tour to Australia, H H played his first match of the 1862 season for the All England Eleven against XXII of the Sheffield (York) Club on the Endcliffe Ground at Sheffield. The team then travelled to Rossall School, situated between Cleveleys and Fleetwood in Lancashire. Here they faced a team of Past and Present Rossallians strengthened by the inclusion of three professionals – J Chatterton, Isaac Hodgson and William Slinn. H H's presence caught the public imagination for 'special trains were run to stop at the end of Rossall Lane and tickets for the three-day match were sold for half-a-crown.'[1]

The Eleven won by eight wickets and 'having given this fine practical lesson to the Rossall gentlemen they hastened back to Yorkshire'[2] whilst H H travelled south for the start of the first county game of the season, against Yorkshire at Kennington Oval. This was the start of a hectic programme of matches for H H. He played in 21 non first-class matches for the All England Eleven plus 16 first-class matches for Surrey and other representative sides.

H H was appointed cricket coach at Rossall School in 1862 and there followed several successful seasons for the school under his guidance. It was the captain of the school cricket team who engaged and paid for the coach at Rossall. The appointment can only have been effective in early spring because of H H's playing commitments from mid-May each year.

Success as a batsman

H H's ability with the bat was widely acclaimed by his fellow professionals.

Richard Daft found that 'Stephenson's play was remarkable for its uprightness. His driving on the on-side was magnificent and he also hit beautifully to square-leg.'[3] William Caffyn noted that 'His off-play for so great a player was undoubtedly weak; nor can I call to mind a batsman who scored so heavily as he did, who was so little noted for his cutting. His defence was very strong, and he always played with a remarkably straight bat.'[4]

Despite these positive remarks it must be said that H H's achievements with the bat were steady rather than spectacular in first-class matches in the early years of his career. His highest aggregate of runs was 390 in 1857, but this was achieved in thirty innings at an average of only 13.93. This was to change in 1862 when his aggregate for the season reached 565 runs at an average of 25.68. His good form continued in 1864 when he recorded two centuries, scoring a total of 824 runs in first-class matches and finishing second in the national batting averages. His innings of 119 against Nottinghamshire at Kennington Oval in early July was the highest score of his career. Another successful season in 1865 saw him record the third century of his career – 110 v Hampshire at Kennington Oval in mid-August.

H H's milestone of 7,000 runs in first-class cricket was reached in the county match against Middlesex at West Brompton in May 1871.

Appearances for the Vale of Evesham Club

Whilst serving as huntsman for the Duc d'Aumale and residing in Fladbury, H H seized the opportunity to play occasionally for the Vale of Evesham Cricket Club whose ground was in the nearby village of Wyre Piddle.[5] Other cricket clubs were in existence in the same area at that time, notably at Evesham and the Vale of Evesham and also at Broadway, a village to the south-east of Evesham. It appears that the Vale of Evesham Club drew its players from the wider locality whereas Evesham Cricket Club selected its players from the town itself.[6]

H H's appearances for the Vale of Evesham aroused much interest and, as the following scorecards show, his performances did not disappoint. In the second innings of the match against Tewkesbury he excelled with a score of 43 not out. On 17 September 1864 *The Evesham Journal* reported that the day's proceedings reached a pleasant conclusion when players and friends adjourned after the match to The Star Hotel in Pershore for 'a first-rate dinner':

A match was commenced yesterday, between eleven of the Vale of Evesham Club, and eleven of the Tewkesbury Club. Considerable interest was manifested in the game owing to H. H. Stephenson, one of the renowned All England Eleven, being engaged on the part of the Evesham and a strong team present on the part of the Tewkesbury. We are unable from want of time and space to give any further details of the game than the full score of the first innings of either side, which was as follows:—

Evesham.—FIRST INNINGS.

A. Haynes, b Dobbs	3
J. B. Whichton, c Causton, b Dobbs	7
H. H. Stephenson, c Dobbs, b Bullock	0
G. Eaden, h w, b Bullock	0
W. P. Byrch, b Bullock	1
H. Haynes, not out	0
Randell, b Dobbs	3
W. Eaden, b Bullock	1
Bullock, c Rice, b Bullock	2
Cox, c Causton, b Dobbs	0
B. George, b Dobbs	1
Byes 3, l b 1	4
	37

Tewkesbury.—FIRST INNINGS.

T. Green, b Byrch	0
Dobbs, c H. H. Stephenson, b Cox	0
Causton, b Byrch	11
Knight, c Eaden, b Stephenson	19
Guilding, run out	0
Bullock, b Byrch	5
Rice, st Byrch, b Stephenson	7
Warren, b Byrch	2
Bishop, not out	0
Gannoway, run out	0
Holding, c H. Haynes, b Stephenson	2
Byes 1, leg-bye 1	2
	48

In the second innings of the Evesham eleven Mr. Whichton obtained 8 runs—H. Haynes, 12—Stephenson (not out) 43—G. Eaden, 0—Byrch, 14—A. Haynes, 3—Randell, 3—W. Eaden, 0—Bullock, 3—Cox, 1—and George, 11—Byes, &c., 9.—Total 107.

In the second innings of Tewkesbury Mr. Dobbs made, 0—Knight, 0—Green, 0—Causton, 8—Guilding, 0—Bullock, 5—Rice, 1—Warren, 0—Bishop, 1—Gannoway, 0—and Holding, 0—Byrch, &c., 0. Total, 30.

The game thus ended in favor of the Evesham with 66 runs to spare.

Mr. D. Chandler, of Tewkesbury, and Mr. F. Foster, acted as umpires. At the conclusion of the game, the players and several of their friends adjourned to the Star Hotel, where a first-rate dinner was provided by Mr. and Mrs. Butler, whose catering was of the best and gave every satisfaction.

This same newspaper stated that agreement had been reached for the opening of the Evesham and Ashchurch Railway in October 1864 for passenger traffic, and it is evident

that good communication by rail enabled local cricket fixtures to take place on a regular basis. The following details of a match at Moreton-in-Marsh, in which H H had played for the Vale of Evesham, appeared in *The Evesham Journal* on 20 May 1865:

A match was played at Moreton on Tuesday last, the 16th inst., between the Moreton and Vale of Evesham clubs, which ended in favour of the latter by one innings and 13 runs. The following was the score:—

MORETON.

1st Innings.		2nd Innings.	
J. B. Wilson c Bullock b Byrch	16	c Byrch	2
T. Pearson b Byrch	0	run out	3
W. Fisher b Byrch	2	b Travis	0
G. Bennett B. Byrch	0	c Bullock	5
Rev. N. Nisbet l b. w., b Travis	15	b Travis	5
E. T. Godman b Travis	0	b Travis	0
Rev. J. W. Sharp b Byrch	10	c Bullock	0
A. C. Rawlinson b Travis	0	b Myatt	0
Rev. F. T. Pendley b Byrch	0	b Myatt	3
G. C. Notley b Byrch	0	not out	6
H. J. Phillips not out	1	b Byrch	7
Byes 9, leg byes 2, wides 1	12	Byes 3, l b. 1, w. 1	5
	56		36

EVESHAM, 1st Innings.

C. A. P. Bullock c Sharp b Fisher	2
P. Myatt l b w, b Sharp	0
W. Byrch c Fisher b Bennett	25
Rev. W. Bristow c Wilson b Wilson	28
H. H. Stephenson b Bennett	16
F. Myatt l b w, b Bennett	6
A. Haynes b Bennett	0
W. Myatt c Fisher b Wilson	5
J. Randell not out	3
J. Travis b Bennett	4
D. Workman b Wilson	2
Byes 5, wides 9	14
	105

The impact of W G Grace

W G Grace made an immediate impact upon the cricketing world in June 1864, just before his sixteenth birthday, by scoring 170 and 50 not out for South Wales against the Gentlemen of Sussex at Hove.

The following year, playing for the Gentlemen of the South against the Players of the South at Kennington Oval, in his first first-class match, W G was stumped by H H before he had scored any runs: 'In the next over from Bennett W G played forward to the second ball, overbalanced and was adroitly stumped by Stephenson (as *The Daily Telegraph* stated: "H H Stephenson was down upon him in excellent form").'[7] W G Grace gained some revenge by dismissing H H for 5, caught at point, in the second innings. Indeed, W G Grace's bowling had much to commend it, as he had match figures of 54.2-23-84-13.

The changing fortunes of Surrey

Surrey remained the most affluent of the county cricket clubs, with an annual income that enabled it to arrange an extensive programme of matches. In 1864 the club played eight county matches, won six of these and drew two, so that when an unofficial county championship table was drawn up, Surrey were declared champions. The club had a poor playing record in 1866 and their decline continued the following year.

For H H the county fixture against Yorkshire at Bramall Lane, Sheffield, was a low point in his life. Surrey were decisively beaten by seven wickets within two days, and on the second day of this match, 28 June 1870, H H heard that his mother, Catherine Stephenson, had died at Fladbury at 66 years of age, of heart disease (according to the death certificate).[8]

Surrey's decline continued in 1871 when, with a side of ageing professionals, they lost nine and drew four of their first-class county matches. It was felt that 'the cause of ill success…was the retention of professionals past their best, or out of form.'[9]

A benefit match

H H had served his county for 18 years and the committee of the Surrey County Cricket Club agreed that a South v North match should be played for his benefit. Attendance figures for the three days of the match were approximately 17,000.[10]

In such matches the beneficiary paid all the expenses but kept all the gate receipts, so we can assume that H H received a handsome financial reward. In the game W G Grace grabbed all the headlines with his batting: in the first innings he was dismissed first ball but in the second innings he redeemed himself by scoring 268 runs. As a result the Surrey Club presented W G with 'a new bat, inscribed suitably on a gold plate, as well as the ball that he hit about to such an extent, as an acknowledgement of the greatness of the feat.'[11]

Conclusion

The award of a benefit match was a fitting tribute to H H Stephenson, whose 18 years of loyal service as one of the country's leading all-rounders helped bring success to the county of Surrey. He was a popular cricketer, and his dignity and sense of fair play had earned him the respect of fellow professionals and amateurs alike.

[1] Bennett, P W, *A Very Definite Position*, Grosvenor Ltd., Blackpool, 1992, p.126
[2] *Lillywhite's Guide to Cricketers*, Spring Edition, 1863, London, p.55
[3] Daft, Richard, *Kings of Cricket: anecdotes and reminiscences from 1858 to 1892*, Tillotson & Son, Bolton, 1893, pp.75-6
[4] Caffyn, William, *Seventy-one not out: the reminiscences of William Caffyn*, William Blackwood & Sons, Edinburgh and London, 1899, p.90
[5] Bradshaw, Ted and Shaw, Bob, *A History of Evesham Cricket Club*, Evesham Cricket Club, Evesham, 2004, p.5
[6] *ibid.*, p.6
[7] Webber, J R, *The Chronicle of W G*, Association of Cricket Statisticians and Historians, West Bridgford, 1998, p.44
[8] Certified Copy of Death Certificate of Catherine Stephenson, in author's possession
[9] Alverstone, Lord and Alcock, C W, *Surrey Cricket – its history and associations*, Longmans, Green and Co., London, 1902, p.152
[10] *M C C Cricket Scores and Biographies*, vol. XII: 1871-1873, Longmans & Co., London, 1879, p.203
[11] Lillywhite, John, *John Lillywhite's Cricketers' Companion*, John Lillywhite, London, 1871, p.54

10. A NEW CHALLENGE

The Uppingham School Cricket Pavilion on the Upper

H H Stephenson's ability as an all-round cricketer and his stature as a respected gentleman, proven leader of men and a sound communicator led to his permanent appointment as cricket coach at Uppingham School, Rutland, in 1872.

Planning for the future

Professional cricketers were often treated as heroes as they travelled to games at provincial grounds with the travelling Elevens, but the financial rewards never matched such importance and fame. Benefit matches were arranged to reward the loyalty of long-serving players but this did not guarantee a secure financial future.

Many players, in fact, fell upon hard times: the Nottinghamshire fast bowler, John Jackson, and Edward Pooley, the Surrey wicket-keeper, died destitute in workhouses, whilst William Mudie died from paralysis of the brain when only 35 years of age.[1] Others, however, were more successful and accepted positions as coaches at public schools or universities.

H H had saved some money and, with his days as a professional county

cricketer drawing to a close, he planned to set up in business in London. He considered that his fame as a cricketer and huntsman would serve him well in that capacity.

The status of cricket at Uppingham School

The appointment of the Rev Edward Thring as Headmaster in 1853 saw an increase in cricketing activity at Uppingham. School fixtures were played against Rockingham Park, Stamford, Harborough and Oundle School, whilst an annual match against the Old Boys was established in 1857. At that time it was normal practice for masters to be included in the school Eleven, and the Headmaster and the Usher, W J Earle, appeared for several years until the school was large enough to dispense with their services.[2] Umpiring the school matches was Tom Aris who 'always appeared in a black swallow-tail dress-coat and a tall silk hat.'[3]

Thring was keen to see his cricketers test their strength against another public school, and the challenge was accepted by Rossall which had a sound reputation for cricket. The match was played there on 25 and 26 May 1863, resulting in victory for Uppingham by nine wickets, with C E Green scoring 87 runs and then taking eight wickets in the match.[4] En route the coach in which they were travelling 'was over-driven and collapsed in a hedge'[5] so that the journey had to be completed by train, with their luggage reaching them some hours later. The hospitality was excellent: 'an old-fashioned arrangement of meals – a biscuit or so in the middle of the day, dinner at four and supper at nine.'[6] Sadly this fixture was not repeated but it was replaced by one against Repton.

The position of cricket professional at Uppingham began in 1864, in alternate years and for just a few weeks in April and May. Frank Silcock was followed by Roger Iddison of Yorkshire in 1866 and Edgar Willsher in 1868 and 1870.[7] However, Thring did not want to see cricket assuming too much importance within the school, so he resisted making a permanent appointment.

Mr C E Green intervenes

Mr C E Green

Charles Ernest Green came to Uppingham in April 1858 when just under 12 years of age, played for the School Eleven for six seasons and was appointed captain in 1864. He was a fine all-rounder and passionate about cricket

at Uppingham. He was a founder member in 1863 of the Uppingham Rovers Cricket Club, a team created 'so that boys and old boys could get together in the holidays for matches.'[8] After leaving Uppingham he played for Cambridge University for the next four seasons, captaining the side in 1868.

Maintaining close contact with cricket at Uppingham, Green persuaded Thring to employ a professional at the school and even guaranteed to pay the salary at the outset. It was Green, in fact, who recommended H H for the position. Green had seen him in action as a coach at Rossall and had frequently faced him when playing for Cambridge University, the Gentlemen or Middlesex. He also shared with H H a love of hunting.

Initially H H had some misgivings about the offer as he thought that such a move was going to dash all his hopes and opportunities for the future; he could never have foreseen how happy and successful he would be as coach at Uppingham School.

H H Stephenson's early years at Uppingham

H H arrived in Uppingham in readiness for the 1872 cricket season. His influence on the structure of cricket throughout the school was felt immediately. It was soon reported that 'Cricket is in a flourishing condition at Uppingham where H H Stephenson has taken up his quarters, and is teaching the boys some of that straight play for which he is so famous.'[9]

Attending to every aspect of the game throughout the school, he did not restrict his attention to members of the First Eleven. Practice nets were organised for the various Elevens, but he insisted on separating his own net from the rest in order to avoid accidents. H H invited just one of the regular bowlers at a time to his net so that he could give him more personal attention, whilst younger boys were openly encouraged to come and field at his net for half an hour, as he lay great importance on fielding and catching.[10]

He instilled in his batsmen the need to play straight, rather than across the line of the ball, and should the ball be pitched on or outside the leg stump he instructed them to play the ball firmly off their legs along the ground between square leg and mid-on. This push shot was soon adopted by the boys and became immediately identifiable as the Uppingham stroke. His enthusiasm for the game became infectious among the pupils, who saw that a style of play was being developed by which Uppingham cricketers could be recognised.[11]

H H arrived at Uppingham School at a very opportune moment as the Eleven was blessed with a nucleus of highly talented batsmen – especially A P Lucas, W S Patterson and D Q Steel. In 1872 Uppingham amassed a total of 374 against Haileybury, with Patterson scoring 116. The visitors were heavily defeated by an innings and 250 runs.

W S Patterson

This resounding victory led Thring to write in his diary for 28 May: 'I don't want the cricket to get too powerful in the school here, and to be worshipped and made the end of life for a

considerable section of the school.'[12] It was reported that six members of the Eleven had gathered in a praepostor's study and 'made claret cup', and in his entry for 29 May Thring wrote: 'This is one of the most utter acts of treason and mock manly meanness I have ever had to deal with…The deliberate, quiet, lying betrayal of trust by leaders in the school. I greatly fear it belongs to the professional and cricket as a science, and the setting up a rival power in the school by having so much made of a thing not taught by a master.' Fortunately, the matter was speedily resolved, with Thring able to proclaim 'a most happy victory of truth and right'.[13]

With H H at the helm and the standard of cricket noticeably improving, a more impressive fixture list was arranged for his second season. At home there were victories against M C C and Ground thanks to some fine batting by Lucas, Patterson, Schultz and Steel, but a first appearance at Kennington Oval against Surrey Club and Ground resulted in defeat by nine wickets.

Any doubts that Thring may have harboured about the importance cricket was assuming in the school were by now allayed. H H became popular with both masters and boys, and when his appointment as a resident professional coach was made permanent he must have felt a debt of gratitude to Mr Green. The Cricket and Football Accounts for 1873 show that H H was receiving a salary of £75, with the professional bowler being paid £28.[14]

An outstanding feature of the M C C match in 1874 was the opening stand of 271, with Lucas scoring 134 and Fleming 163 runs, whilst Fleming demonstrated his consistency with a score of 118 against an Eleven brought down by G H Longman, the Cambridge University captain.[15]

In 1875 the Eleven played for the first time at Lord's, where they defeated the M C C by six runs in a single innings game. The Repton match ended in victory for Uppingham by an innings and 220 runs, with T M Patterson playing a magnificent innings of 165. With such a talented array of batsmen who could be called upon each year, these were halcyon days for cricket in Uppingham.

Married life in Uppingham

On 16 July 1873 in the Parish Church of Esher, H H married Maria Willbe Horwood, who was 33 years of age, the daughter of John Horwood, a butcher, and his wife Mary.[16] H H's popularity among the exiled French royal family ensured that several members of the Duc d'Aumale's household travelled from France to witness the ceremony.

H H and his wife then rented a house in High Street West in Uppingham. As well as being a professional cricket coach he became a cricketing and sports outfitter, making flannels and caps for the boys. Equally, members of the Uppingham Rovers Club could obtain the Rover flannel and ribbons from H H and have coats and caps made up by him.

He is also described as an insurance agent,[17] and even as a coal agent,[18] positions which would supplement his meagre income a little.

The births of Rose Alice Osborne on 16 July 1874 and of Frances Mary on 25 December 1876 brought much joy to H H and his wife. Their happiness was complete with the arrival of Heathfield Harman on 23 March 1881.[19] The birthdays of their daughters were quite significant: Rose's birthday coincided with the wedding anniversary of her parents, and Frances was born on Christmas Day.

In 1873 H H continued to play for the United South of England Eleven in non first-class matches during the school holidays, at Leicester, Wakefield and Coventry. He also joined the ranks of the XXII of Uppingham who beat the United North of England Eleven by six wickets.

On 13 July 1874 H H played alongside W G Grace against XXII of Hornsea in the East Riding where a large crowd had gathered to see W G, 'popularly known as the "leviathan" amongst cricketers', and 'to witness the batting, bowling, and fielding of, perhaps, the most wonderful cricketer that ever took bat in hand.'[20] The demands placed upon such cricketers are exemplified by the fact that Messrs. Grace, Silcock and Stephenson were obliged to leave Hornsea in the mid-morning of the Wednesday in order to reach Dublin for the match beginning the following morning against XXII of Leinster. Consequently H H was far from home when daughter Rose was born. His final appearances for the United South of England Eleven were at Leicester and Birmingham in 1875.

Exile in Borth

Problems involving the water supply, drainage and sanitation in Uppingham led to an outbreak of typhoid at Uppingham School in the autumn of 1875. This affected boys in six school houses, leading to the deaths of four pupils and the son of a housemaster. In the town Dr Bell reported that twelve of his patients, including H H, were suffering from fever symptoms, but that these were not serious.[21] When a further outbreak occurred in the spring of 1876, Thring decided to move the staff and pupils to Borth, situated on the coast north of Aberystwyth in Wales, and H H accompanied them.

H H Stephenson's House at Borth

The large cricket roller was transported by rail from Uppingham and was used on a piece of land that the school rented from Sir Pryse Pryse on his estate at Gogerddan so that cricket matches might be played there. That summer, school fixtures were played at Repton and Shrewsbury, but not at Haileybury.[22]

Meanwhile, back in Uppingham, a new water supply had been created, the drains cleaned and repaired, and the school was warmly welcomed back by the townspeople, particularly the tradesmen, in May 1877.

Conclusion

A happily married man, H H Stephenson made an immediate impression upon the cricketing scene at Uppingham School, where he commanded respect and loyalty, instilling in his boys a sense of the serious nature of the game. He nurtured and developed the cricketing talents of so many pupils who recognised how indebted they were to their teacher.

A P Lucas

[1] Bailey, Philip; Thorn, Philip and Wynne-Thomas, Peter, *Who's Who of Cricketers*, Hamlyn, London, 1992, p.756
[2] Patterson, William S, *Sixty Years of Uppingham Cricket*, Longmans, Green and Co., London, 1909, p.49
[3] *ibid.*, p.18
[4] *M C C Cricket Scores and Biographies*, vol.VIII: 1863-1864, Longmans & Co., London, 1877, p.31
[5] Patterson, William S, *Sixty Years of Uppingham Cricket*, p.27
[6] *ibid.*, p.27
[7] Tozer, Malcolm, 'The First of the Great School Coaches' in *The Journal of the Cricket Society*, vol. XVII: Autumn, London, 1994, p.16
[8] *ibid.*, p.16
[9] *John Lillywhite's Cricket Annual for 1873*, London, 1874, pp.23-4
[10] Patterson, William S, *Sixty Years of Uppingham Cricket*, p.71
[11] *ibid.*, p.78
[12] Parkin, G R, *Life and Letters of Edward Thring*, Macmillan & Co. Ltd., London, 1900, p.195
[13] *ibid.*, p.196
[14] *Uppingham School Magazine*, March 1874, p.69
[15] *ibid.*, November 1874, p.295
[16] Certified Copy of Marriage Certificate, in author's possession
[17] *Kelly's Directory of Leicestershire and Rutland, 1881*, Kelly and Co., London, 1881, p.762
[18] *C N Wright's Directory of Leicestershire and Rutland, 1896*, Tompkin and Shardlow, Leicester, 1896, p.766
[19] Certified Copies of these Birth Certificates, in author's possession
[20] *The Hull and Eastern Counties Herald*, 16 July 1874
[21] Richardson, Nigel, *Typhoid in Uppingham: Analysis of a Victorian Town and School in Crisis 1875-1877*, Pickering & Chatto, London, 2008, p.86
[22] Patterson, William S, *Sixty Years of Uppingham Cricket*, p.99

11. A FEW REMARKS ON CRICKET

At Uppingham School cricket continued to flourish under the careful and principled guidance of H H Stephenson, whose extensive cricketing abilities, both practical and theoretical, were highly regarded by all.

Cambridge Blues

Uppingham cricket under H H attracted further attention in 1876 when, in the Varsity match, four members of the victorious Cambridge side were Uppinghamians – namely A P Lucas, H T L Luddington, W S Patterson and D Q Steel. Luddington and Patterson took sixteen wickets, whilst the four Old Uppinghamians contributed a total of 225 runs, with Patterson scoring an undefeated 105 in his only innings.

The following year, 1877, was the Golden Jubilee Year of the Varsity Match and, with S S Schultz gaining selection for Cambridge, Uppingham's representatives now numbered five. Patterson captained the side in 1877 when he and Luddington were responsible for all ten Oxford wickets that fell.[1]

Of these illustrious players, Lucas played for England in five Tests against Australia and Schultz played in one.[2]

Uppingham School Eleven, 1878

Steel, Patterson and Schultz also played for Lancashire, and Lucas qualified either by birth or residence to play for Surrey, Middlesex and Essex.

Some sobering thoughts

The year in Borth may have unsettled the discipline and cohesion of the Eleven, for they were unable to reach the exalted standards of previous years. The batting was now unreliable but the bowling had acquired greater penetration with the emerging talent of Hugh Rotherham, who took over 100 wickets in 1878.

That same year a note of dissension appeared in the *Uppingham School Magazine* from a boy who asserted: 'We are justly proud of the distinction which the School has won in the practice of the "noble art" but…we cannot but feel that this success represents only the high training of a section, and that not a large one, of the School.' He complained of 'the increasing tendency to make Cricket a profession, and every cricketer a specialist', concluding that 'If Cricketers wish to make the game their profession and object in life, by all means let them do so, but let them not check others from simple enjoyment of a delightful game by giving it claims superior to all other considerations of work and daily life.'[3]

A word or two from the coach

Beginning in 1879, H H used the *Uppingham School Magazine* each year as a vehicle for passing on his advice to succeeding generations of boys, missing no opportunity to inspire them with 'a few remarks on cricket'.

The following letter on the subject of fielding and bowling appeared in the School Magazine of April 1880. It shows the very thorough theoretical approach that he employed in order to articulate the principles of the game to all the boys:

CORRESPONDENCE.

(The Editors decline to hold themselves responsible for the opinions of their Correspondents.)

TO THE EDITOR OF THE "UPPINGHAM SCHOOL MAGAZINE."

Sir,

About this time last year you were kind enongh to insert in the School Magazine a letter from me on the subject of fielding at cricket. I was very pleased to see that my letter had some effect, and I am induced to ask you for a small amount of space again this year, to remind the cricketers of the School that they are very far from being perfect in that department, and to impress on them that they must not forget the lesson I asked them to learn last year, viz., that they mnst always keep up a lively feeling, and not be half asleep; and that they must never by any chance wait until the ball comes to them, but must make a rush to meet it; and at the same time collect themselves in such a manner as to be able to throw the ball either to the bowler or wicket-keeper without losing time. When at a short distance from the wicket, the ball should be thrown straight into the hands of the bowler or wicket-keeper; but if the fielder is a long distance from the wicket, the ball should be made to hit the ground first, so that it reaches the hand as a "long-hop." Especial care must be taken to throw the ball to the *top* of the wicket. *Never*, if it can be avoided, throw the ball to the bottom of the stumps. I make this repetition of my last year's remarks, because I know that there are many here now who were not then. There certainly was *some* improvement in the fielding on the Middle Ground last season, and I have no doubt that, if the weather had been fine, it would have been still more noticeable. I mention the Middle Ground because that is our nursery for cricket, and if we can only instil the right form and style *there*, they will find it much easier, when they come to the Upper Ground.

Now I want to say a few words about bowling. I notice in nearly all cases that the first thing that ought to be studied in bowling is the last that is even thought of. I mean LENGTH. If a ball is a good *length*, the batsman can't make anything off it, even if it is not straight; and he is very likely to be caught out in trying to hit it. Length varies according to the pace of the bowler. If medium pace, the ball must be pitched farther up than is necessary for a fast bowler. A medium-pace bowler must pitch the ball from $4\frac{1}{2}$ to 5 yards from the wicket; a fast bowler from $5\frac{1}{2}$ to 6. But a great deal must depend upon the reach of the batsman you are bowling to. If a man has a long reach, it stands to reason that you must pitch your ball shorter than you would to a small man. To bowl a good length you should fix your eye on something near the spot where you think the ball ought to pitch. There is always a daisy, a blade of grass, or something of the sort, that you can use as a mark. Keep your eye on that spot; try to pitch the ball on it, and your hand and eye are sure to work together. Be careful not to bowl above your strength; by so doing you will have far greater command over the ball, and will be able to alter your pace and pitch according to the batsman's play. Keep your *hand and arm* as high as possible.

I seldom see anyone trying to bowl "lobs." There is no bowling more useful in a School Eleven. With fielding, *as School fielding ought to be*, a lob bowler is sure to get a great many wickets. I offered, my first year, to give a new bat to anyone who would come out as a good slow "lob" bowler, and I repeat the offer now. I hope it will not be supposed that I have mentioned fielding and bowling as being the only departments at cricket in which the School is deficient. I could mention many other things that ought to be much more studied than they are at present, but I have already taken up a great deal of your space.

I am, Sir, yours, etc.,
H. H. STEPHENSON.

As a former professional cricketer, H H was able to back up his words of advice by reference to his own experiences. He happily recalled in an interview a remarkable catch that he once took: 'I remember that once at Leicester a ball came towards me at long-leg. I started for it without the least hopes of reaching it, but the wind turned it, and I brought off a catch which Clarke said was the finest he had seen.'[4]

To prevent round-arm bowling, boys were taught to bowl by standing close to a wall. They had to move their arm high and in a circle to avoid grazing their knuckles. He encouraged bowlers to aim at a small object on the wicket or just outside the off stump and to concentrate on a good length.

H H's expertise as a coach extended to 'Notes' which he made on his own copy of *The Cricket-Field*, a book written by James Pycroft in 1851. One of the classics of cricket literature, this book was re-printed on several occasions and its last edition appeared in 1922 incorporating H H's 'Notes'. In it H H offers similar advice to the above but uses different imagery, now alluding to the world of shooting: 'The rifleman picks a spot on a stag's shoulder and the sportsman picks out a particular bird rather than firing indiscriminately into a covey of partridges; so the bowler should pick out a small spot between himself and the wicket.'[5]

For the batsman H H recommends in these 'Notes' that the blade of the bat be raised about half a foot from the ground as soon as the bowler begins to advance so as to screen the stumps from the bowler's eye. He encourages the batsman to take guard on the crease and then stand two feet in front of it – so long as the wicket-keeper is not standing up to the wicket. In addition he advocates the use of an oval handle, warning against the use of a bat with a round handle as it may turn edgeways in the hand without the batsman's knowledge.[6]

Umpiring

H H's all-round interest and participation in cricket extended to his role as an umpire in 14 first-class matches (cf. Appendix 5, p.64). Until the M C C drew up an official list of umpires in 1887 it was the responsibility of a county to nominate an umpire for a match. Consequently most games in which H H officiated took place at Kennington Oval.

He had the distinction of standing as umpire in the first Test Match to be played in England between England and Australia at Kennington Oval, beginning on 6 September 1880. England won by five wickets, with W G Grace scoring 152 in his first innings. Playing alongside him were his brothers, Edward and Fred, the first instance of three brothers playing in the same Test Match.[7] A P Lucas scored 55, sharing in a stand of 120 with W G; but in the second innings it is said that Lucas was given out by H H, caught at the wicket, when the ball had hit his pad.[8]

H H regularly umpired school matches. It was generally accepted that he did not help the boys with advice during the game. However, Stanley Christopherson, an Old Boy, relates an anecdote which suggests that he was not averse to doing so when the occasion demanded: 'Once when I took down a team I noticed that though he was umpiring he did not say much to the boys. Presently a fly got in his eye, and he went up to one of the boys, who apparently took it out. But the boy moved to another place, and I think he caught a man directly afterwards. The fly still continued to trouble H H, and a boy always moved after he had inspected the eye.'[9]

Uppingham Rovers Cricket Club

The Rules of the Rover Club state that Members are elected annually from those boys who have played with 'especial cricket merit' in the Uppingham School Eleven. The Club was inaugurated on 24 June 1864 with a match against The Rugby Club,[10] and from that early date it could count upon around 70 members. Each year members gathered for a Rover Tour in the South – including a match at Esher – and this concluded with a dinner in London. From 1871 matches were played against sides such as Leicestershire and the Gentlemen of Warwickshire.

The Uppingham Rovers were able to field very strong sides made up almost entirely of county and England players. Their games attracted good crowds and were followed daily by a representative of the Central Press Association, so the doings of the Rovers were known far and wide. Consequently their records became known as 'The Doings of the Uppingham Rovers'. One member was known as the 'Rhyming Rover'. Every year he produced a song which was sung heartily at the annual dinner and was always set to the tune of another well known song of the time. In 1876 his song was called 'The Uppingham Blues' and it included the following verse:

'Who taught them this excellent cricket?
Was the question of many that day.
Who taught them to keep up their wicket,
And to hit just as well as they play?
Oh, who did these cricketers nourish?
Who trained their eyes, nerves and thews?
Twas STEPHENSON! Long may he flourish!
The coach of the Uppingham Blues!'[11]

From an early time in his life at Uppingham H H was invited to umpire for the Rovers on their annual tours, but his first appearance in a game was in fact playing against the Rovers for Stamford in 1874 and 1875. The first volume of 'The Doings' contains an amusing piece entitled 'An Intercepted Letter From A Lady Rover', dated September 1882, describing how the writer's husband had

taken her on the Rovers tour and how charming she had found the Rovers. Describing its members, she says: 'I must not forget Mr H H Stephenson, who umpired, and always gave *Mr Green in* when he was *out*, and *Mr Street out* when he was *in*. He is such a nice man, and so attentive to us ladies. Much of the Rover success, Tom says, is due to the trouble he takes to teach the Uppingham boys to play good cricket.'[12]

The reputation and playing records of the Rovers at that time were, of course, attributed to the remarkable ability of H H, whose coaching continued to produce such fine cricketers.

Changing scene of cricket in the town

The presence of such a cricketing personality as H H did much to generate interest in the game amongst the townspeople. *The Lincoln, Rutland and Stamford Mercury* tells us that a new cricket club was formed in 1872 as a result of 'the early closing and Saturday half-holiday movement' and that the club played on an excellent ground about two-thirds of a mile from the town (Van Diemen's Land).[13] During Feast Week, held in the second week of July 1873, over 3,000 people paid admission to watch the two-day match there between the Uppingham Victoria Cricket Club and Messrs. King and Casey's Clowns.[14]

With the school away at Borth, Thring put the school cricket ground at the disposal of the Uppingham Victoria Cricket Club in 1876, and he was elected President of the Club in 1877. During Feast Week in 1877, the first Display of Fruit and Flowers was held on the Upper Cricket Ground on Seaton Road. On the following day, 12 July, H H assembled a strong team comprising masters, Old Boys and local players who beat a Derbyshire side by nine wickets:

UPPINGHAM.			
FIRST INNINGS.		**SECOND INNINGS.**	
Mr. A. P. Lucas, b Tatlow	1	not out	13
Mr. A. Ackroyd, b Platts	13	b Hind	4
J. E. Steel, 1-b-w, b Tatlow	23		
Mr. J. B. Maul, b Platts	0		
H. H. Stephenson, c J. Cooke, b Tatlow	4		
Mr. D. Q. Steel, run out	37		
Mr. J. H. M. Hare, b Hind	62		
Mr. W. C. Perry, c J. Cooke, b Tatlow	32		
Mr. S. S. Schultz, c and b E. Cooke	0	not out	10
F. Wright, 1-b-w, b E. Cooke	9		
Mr. J. G. Thring, b E. Cooke	0		
Rev. A. J. Tuck, 1-b-w, b Platts	2		
J. N. Frisby, 1-b-w, b Tatlow	19		
W. H. Ingram, c Frost, b Tatlow	0		
W. Goodwin, c E. Cooke, b Hind	0		
A. Waugh, c Smith, b Tatlow	0		
H. Drake, b Hind	0		
W. Brown, not out	0		
Extras	29	Extras	1
Total	231	Total	28

DERBYSHIRE.			
Mr. J. B. Oakley, 1-b-w, b Maul	3	c Frisby, b D. Q. Steel	0
G. Frost, c Stephenson, b Maul	23	b Maul	1
W. Rigley, b Maul	1	c Schultz, b D. Q. Steel	24
Mr. R. P. Smith, c Wright, b Ackroyd	29	c Perry, b Lucas	34
T. Foster, c Maul, b Lucas	10	c Stephenson, b Lucas	10
J. Platts, st. D. Q. Steel, b Lucas	52	c Ackroyd, b D. Q. Steel	1
A. Hind, c Ackroyd, b Stephenson	41	not out	6
E. Cooke, c Steel, b Lucas	3	b Maul	3
H. Shaw, not out	4	c Lucas, b Maul	0
Mr. E. Tatlow, b Stephenson	0	c Goodwin, b Maul	2
J. Cooke b Stephenson	1	run out	0
Extras	5	Extras	4
Total	172	Total	85

Uppingham School Magazine, October 1877, p.289

It was undoubtedly the renown of H H that brought such a fixture to Uppingham. In 1878 he was elected to the committee of the Victoria Club, and the ground was placed under his management.[15]

At the A G M in 1881 members of the Uppingham and District Club presented an album of photographs to the Rev Edward Thring, their President, 'as a token of their esteem for him as a fellow-townsman, and their high appreciation of his great labour and liberality in promoting the physical amusements of "rising" Uppingham, and cricket in particular.'[16]

The Uppingham Town Cricket Club which played on Tod's Piece was by now defunct. The Uppingham and District Cricket Club, meanwhile, at the A G M in 1886, changed its name to the Victoria Club, with H H now a Vice-President.[17]

Highs and Lows

One or two lean years now followed. H H complained of slackness amongst the boys and criticised those who neglected net practice claiming that they had school work to do, but who were in fact seen hanging about, or inside a 'grub shop'.[18] That same year Uppingham suffered defeats against Loretto and Repton, and these represented the first against another school since H H's arrival.

W F Whitwell did much to restore Uppingham's reputation with his 17 wickets against Repton School in 1886. The same period saw the emergence of Gregor MacGregor as a brilliant wicket-keeper who captained Cambridge in 1891 and played in eight Test matches before captaining Middlesex from 1899 until 1907.

Gregor MacGregor
From author's collection

In 1884 further honours came to the school when Lucas, Rotherham and Christopherson played at Lord's in the Gentlemen v Players match. That same year Christopherson played in the Second Test at Lord's when England defeated Australia by an innings and five runs.

48

Although he was wary of cricket assuming too great a prominence in the school, Thring derived much pleasure from Uppingham's successes at cricket. Despite Thring's death in October 1887, H H's enthusiasm for his role was undiminished. In 1890 he organised a cricket tour during the summer holiday, with matches at Esher, Streatham, Tooting and Crystal Palace: 'H H was in tremendous form throughout, and his song of Mr and Mrs Dolus "took the cake."'[19] With the batting of Hemingway and the bowling of Bardswell, the Eleven flourished in 1891, aided by the great all-round talent of C E M Wilson who, after captaining the Cambridge side in 1898, played in two Tests against South Africa.[20] Finally, T L Taylor was captain of the Eleven in 1896 when he achieved a batting average of 84.60. He proceeded to Cambridge and captained their side in 1900. He played successfully for Yorkshire and, in 1901, Wisden made him one of its 'Five Cricketers of the Year'.[21]

Esher and Uppingham School

Links between H H's home town of Esher and Uppingham School were strengthened by the two Martineau families. Mr Philip M Martineau, a barrister of Littleworth House in Esher, had two sons educated at Uppingham. Lionel was a very good all-round cricketer and captained the Eleven in 1885, before gaining his Blue for Cambridge in the Varsity match of 1887. The other son, Charles, played for the Elevens of 1879 and 1880.

Mr George Martineau, a sugar refiner of Buckland House in Esher, had four sons educated at Uppingham School and, with the exception of Arthur who died at the age of 14 years, they all progressed to Cambridge. After his graduation from Trinity College, the eldest son, George, was appointed as an Assistant Master at Uppingham in 1890.

It may be that the Martineau families knew H H from his Esher days and chose Uppingham knowing that H H, with 'his width of experience and knowledge of the world',[22] would keep a fatherly eye on their sons' well-being.

Conclusion

H H Stephenson was instrumental in developing cricket in Uppingham and fostering a healthy relationship between school and town. Throughout his 25 years as the school's cricket coach, he adhered to the principles of the straight bat and good length bowling, and encouraged boys to take a delight in fielding well. The long list of Old Boys who achieved fame in the world of cricket bears testimony to the quality of his coaching (cf. Appendix 6, p.65).

[1] Chesterton, George and Doggart, Hubert, *Oxford and Cambridge Cricket*, Willow Books, London, 1989, pp.90-1
[2] Frindall, Bill, *England Test Cricketers*, Willow Books, London, 1989, pp.287 and 386
[3] *Uppingham School Magazine*, Correspondence, June 1878, p.128
[4] *The Cricket Field*, 1 June 1895, p.141
[5] Pycroft, James, *The Cricket-Field, with some Notes by H H Stephenson*, ed. F S Ashley-Cooper, St James's Press Co. Ltd., London, 1922, p.235
[6] *ibid.*, p.167
[7] Frindall, Bill, *England Test Cricketers*, p.235
[8] Hornung, E W, 'Our Public Schools: XVI – Uppingham' in *Country Life*, 28 July 1917, p.6
[9] Bettesworth, W A, *Chats on the Cricket Field*, Merritt & Hatcher Ltd., London, 1910, p.93
[10] *Uppingham School Magazine*, September 1864, p.263
[11] *The Doings of the Uppingham Rovers*, vol.I
[12] *ibid.*
[13] *The Lincoln, Rutland and Stamford Mercury*, 2 August 1872
[14] *ibid.*, 18 July 1873
[15] *ibid.*, 22 February 1878
[16] *ibid.*, 13 May 1881
[17] *ibid.*, 26 March 1886
[18] *Uppingham School Magazine*, April 1883, p.111
[19] *Supplement to the October School Magazine*, 1890, p.12
[20] Frindall, Bill, *England Test Cricketers*, pp.496-7
[21] Chesterton, George and Doggart, Hubert, *Oxford and Cambridge Cricket*, p.120
[22] Graham, John P, *Forty Years of Uppingham*, Macmillan and Co. Ltd., London, 1932, p.48

CRICKET, FOOTBALL, LAWN TENNIS,

AND ALL OTHER BRITISH SPORTS.

H. ✦ H. ✦ STEPHENSON,

MEMBER OF THE ALL ENGLAND ELEVEN,

(One of the First Eleven who visited America and Australia)

Cricket Coach to the Gentlemen of Uppingham School,

HIGH STREET, UPPINGHAM,

Begs to announce that he has on hand a Well-Seasoned Stock of COBBETT'S

CRICKET BATS,

and all other makers; also

CRICKET BALLS,

Of all makers; and every article connected with the Game of Cricket.

FOOTBALLS,

And everything used in the Game kept in stock.

LAWN TENNIS BATS

Of every description, varying in prices from 7s 6d. to £1. Jeffrie's Lawn Tennis REGULATION BALLS *and* UNCOVERED BALLS *for wet weather.* SHOES *for Ladies and Gentlemen, and everything required for the Game.*

GOLF CLUBS, BALLS,

And everything connected with the Game of Golf.

Agent *for ELLIS and EVERARD, Coal, Coke, Granite, and* Artificial Manure Merchants,

---

Agent to the Royal Exchange Life & Fire Assurance Company.

12. FAMILY AND COMMUNITY

A family man of high integrity and deep religious convictions, H H Stephenson set an example of a practising Christian who saw it as his duty to do his best for school and town, until failing health led to his death in December 1896.

Home and family

Initially H H and his wife rented a house in High Street West (the present-day Westholme) until 1879 when they purchased from Henry Drake, a stonemason, the property next door known as Balmaghie 'comprising all those two messuages, dwellings or tenements with yards thereto adjoining in the West End of High Street.'[1]

The Stephenson family, 1881

From left to right: Frances Mary,
Maria Willbe, Heathfield Harman,
H H, Rose Alice Osborne

According to the 1891 Census, Uppingham's population was 2,559. Mary Cunningham, 16 years of age, and Ellen Naylor, 17, two young servants, were now living in High Street West

with H H, his wife and their two daughters. On the other hand, their son, Heathfield, now 10 years old, was boarding in the High Street in the property of the Headmistress of the Girls' High School, Mary Beisiegel.

Community involvement

Besides his links with the Uppingham Victoria Cricket Club, H H was also a Vice-President of the Uppingham Football Club. He became closely involved with several organisations in the town and was elected to the committee of the Mutual Improvement Society. This had been founded in 1866 to provide cultural entertainment and sporting opportunities for the people of the town.[2] The twelve elected members of the committee comprised prominent citizens together with Masters from Uppingham School. Its President, the Rev Edward Thring, announced in 1880 that membership of the society had reached 390. Music concerts were often given by schoolmaster Paul David and entertainment was frequently provided for the benefit of the funds of the Uppingham Victoria Cricket Club. As part of this same organisation H H was also on the committee of the Literary Institute, where it is reported that 308 members took out 4,608 books during the year.[3]

At the Vestry Meeting held in the Infant School Room on 12 June 1884, H H was made a sidesman at the Parish Church in Uppingham.[4] Further to this he was elected as an overseer of the poor, with the responsibility of paying out money to the poor of the parish from charities administered by the Church.[5]

H H was a member of the committee which organised the first Fat Stock Show in Uppingham on Wednesday 10 December 1890. Following the show the animals were submitted for sale by auction. Afterwards, at the Falcon Hotel, 60 people sat down to a dinner which was presided over by the M P, Mr G H Finch.

H H maintained an active interest in shooting and hunting and was usually in attendance when the Cottesmore Hounds met in the Market Place or at Beaumont Chase.

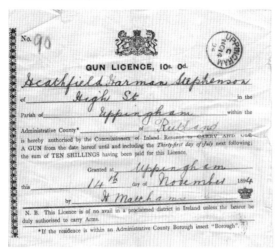

H H's gun licence

An inspiration to others

The family's cricketing tradition was continued by H H's nephew, John Maurice Read. Born at Thames Ditton in 1859, he sustained the high standards of his illustrious relative as an aggressive batsman, playing for Surrey from 1880 until 1895. Like H H he was a popular figure on the cricket field and represented England in 17 Test matches, taking part in four tours to Australia and one to South Africa. Through his nephew, H H was able to maintain a personal interest in the fortunes of Surrey cricket.

In the wider cricketing world, administrators of the game paid H H the compliment of consulting him on matters relating to the laws of cricket. On one occasion Henry Perkins, Secretary of the M C C for 21 years from 1876, requested his advice on a proposed alteration to Law 53 concerning the follow-on. After expressing his measured opinion on the

matter, H H recommended that the decision be left in the hands of Mr Ponsonby, Mr V E Walker and Mr Nicholson 'since you could not put it into the hands of wiser and better than these three.'[6]

Some nearby schools sought H H's assistance, none more so than the Grammar School in Wellingborough, where he was invited to watch games in progress before speaking to the boys 'to find fault where it's wanted, and to encourage as you well know how.' The letter talks of H H in glowing terms: 'The boys here will believe anything that you tell them, and when I tell them that you know more about boys' cricket and the way it should be played than any man living, masters will be only too glad to carry out your instructions and boys to profit by them.'[7]

Devout Christians

The Collins Pocket Diary kept by H H's daughter Frances for 1892 faithfully portrays the daily routines of the members of the family. It shows that they were regular church-goers and that they had their own pew; on several Sundays they attended two or three services. The girls often went to a class for Religious Instruction at the Rectory, and the Ven Archdeacon Lightfoot, the Uppingham Rector, was a frequent visitor to their house.

Personal letters from H H to Frances on her birthdays on Christmas Day lead us to a closer understanding of H H as a father and fervent Christian:

'I pray that God will bless and protect you from all sin and wickedness, and make you a wise and good woman.'[8]

'I hope nothing will happen to drive away from you those good godly ways you possess nor the disposition you seem to have to do his will and please him. Be sure of this, my child, while you rest upon him for help he will never leave you, so mind and be very careful through life who you make friends of

…as soft words and lovely promises are apt to drive the thought of God out of your mind.'[9]

The diary reports that, for his birthday on 3 May 1892, the family gave H H a Prayer Book with his monogram on the front. On her 19th birthday the family's servant Ellen received a Church Service Book.

Health problems

In a letter to Frances dated 7 December 1895, H H describes himself as 'a dreadful old cripple'. For several years he had suffered from nephritis (inflammation of the kidneys). Furthermore, attacks of bronchitis and a troublesome heart made it difficult for him to get his breath. He considered having a lift installed in the house as he was finding it difficult to get up the second flight of stairs to his room.

His customary letter of advice and encouragement to pupils appeared in the School Magazine of June 1896, with the Editor's prefacing comment that 'the hints are as fresh as the spring itself'. He maintained an active interest in the Eleven, his spirits raised by the victory at Repton when C E Wilson scored 201 not out and the captain, T L Taylor, scored 100. Sadly, though, H H felt unable to accompany Rose to the Varsity match at Lord's a few days later as he did not want to be ill away from home.

Farewell

In the latter part of 1896, H H's state of health declined yet further, as the nephritis from which he had been suffering steadily worsened. On 17 December, just as the boys were leaving Uppingham at the end of term, he passed away peacefully, with his daughter Rose at his bedside: 'He too went, in the early morning hours, to his long home; for all was ready, and his work was done.'[10]

Although it was widely known that H H had been ill for some time, the news nonetheless came as a great shock, not least to those school pupils who had left Uppingham that day and who first learned of it in the newspaper at their family home the following morning.

The funeral took place on Monday 21 December. Business premises in the town were closed, and the bells of the Parish Church and the School Chapel tolled as the churchwardens and sidesmen led the procession from the house. The service was conducted by the Ven Archdeacon Lightfoot and the Rev E C Selwyn, Headmaster of Uppingham School. Flags of the School and the Uppingham Rovers Cricket Clubs covered the coffin.

Besides relatives, schoolmasters and leading residents of the town, the funeral was attended by representatives of the Surrey Cricket Club, the Uppingham Victoria Cricket Club, the Cricketers' Fund Benefit Society and a large number of Old Uppinghamians.[11]

Throughout Uppingham, at school and in the town, there was a universal sense of loss at H H's parting. For 25 seasons he had remained loyal and devoted to Uppingham cricket, developing a style of play and a batting technique that became instantly recognisable. Boys and masters admired him as a player for the skills he possessed and could impart to them. They respected and trusted him for his character, personality and high principles arising from his Christian faith. He occupied a unique position at the school.

In the days following H H's death, his widow received many messages of condolence. The sentiment of the time was fully captured in the letter from his former pupil, W S Patterson, in tribute to 'dear old H H':

The Gables.
Fulwood Park
Liverpool.
18 Dec 1896.

Dear Mrs Stephenson,

Will you allow me to add my condolences with yourself and your family to the many you will be receiving. "Dear old H.H" as all of his pupils loved to call him, has gone to his rest amidst the affection & regard of all who met him. and many will like myself. Keenly regret that they will see him no more. for Uppingham will not be the same place without him.

It was not merely his skill in teaching us cricket that made us all love him — and I was his very first pupil at Uppingham & Captain of the XI. but it was his fine character which made everyone — masters. Parents & Boys alike — know that they could depend upon him doing only what was right.

May you have comfort in your sorrow, & may it be some consolation to feel the wide-spread affection & regard that existed for Your Husband & our "dear old H.H"

Yours very sincerely,
William S. Patterson

Letter from William S Patterson to Mrs Stephenson

Conclusion

In his career as a professional cricketer, H H Stephenson excelled as a batsman, bowler, wicket-keeper, captain and coach, and was an occasional umpire at first-class matches. He was ideally suited to leading a touring team into unknown territory, and made history by being the first captain of an English side in Australia. When no longer able to compete at first-class level, he turned his considerable talents to nurturing a new generation of players at Uppingham School, where his impact was legendary. He is regarded by many as one of the most influential cricketing personalities of the Victorian era.

H H Stephenson's tombstone in the Lower Churchyard in Uppingham

The inscription reads:

BELOVED AND REGRETTED BY MASTERS AND BOYS OF UPPINGHAM SCHOOL WHOSE HIGH TRADITIONS HE NOBLY UPHELD FOR 24 YEARS AS A FAMOUS CRICKETER, A WISE TEACHER, AND A LOYAL FRIEND

'More than conquerors through him that loved us'
Romans 9. 37.

[1] *Uppingham Register of Land Values*, Conveyance, 12 February 1879, Record Office for Leicestershire, Leicester & Rutland, DE 2072/216
[2] *The Lincoln, Rutland and Stamford Mercury*, 30 May 1879
[3] *ibid.*, 16 May 1884
[4] *Uppingham Parish Church Churchwardens Account Book*, 1871-1939, Record Office for Leicestershire, Leicester & Rutland, DE 4905/9
[5] *The Lincoln, Rutland and Stamford Mercury*, 4 April 1890
[6] Draft of an undated letter, in the collection of John Oakley
[7] Letter dated 20 July 1895, from Dr H E Platt to 'My Dear H H', in the collection of John Oakley
[8] Letter dated 25 December 1889, in the collection of John Oakley
[9] Letter dated Christmas Day 1893, in the collection of John Oakley
[10] *Uppingham School Magazine*, February 1897, p.3
[11] *The Lincoln, Rutland and Stamford Mercury*, 25 December 1896

APPENDIX 1

Appearances in all first-class matches

	Surrey	England	All England Eleven	South	Players	Players of South	Players of Surrey	Surrey Club	Surrey XI Australia	Single	USEE	South of Thames	Surrey & Sussex	England XI in N. America	Surrey & Middx.	Total
1853	1															1
1854	4	1		1												7
1855	1	1		1												3
1856	3	2														5
1857	7	2	2	3	2								2			18
1858	6	1	2	1	2					1						13
1859	6		2	1	2			2								13
1860	7		2	2	1									1		13
1861	11	2	3	1	1											18
1862	11		1	2	1				1							16
1863	10		1	3	1		1									16
1864	10		1	2	1	1										15
1865	16			2	2	1										21
1866	13			1		1		1				1				17
1867	14					1										15
1868	16					1									1	18
1869	10				1											11
1870	17					1					1					19
1871	16					1										17
	179	9	14	20	14	7	1	4	1	1	1	1	2	1	1	256

APPENDIX 2

Batting averages in all first-class matches

	Matches	Innings	Runs	Not out	Highest Score	Average
1853	1	2	13	1	8*	13.00
1854	7	13	164	2	34*	14.90
1855	3	5	45	1	36	11.25
1856	5	8	139	-	57	17.37
1857	18	30	390	2	51	13.93
1858	13	21	341	2	87	17.09
1859	13	22	280	-	48	12.72
1860	13	23	286	5	30	15.89
1861	18	31	329	-	42	10.61
Australia	1	2	7	-	4	3.50
1862	15	26	565	4	70*	25.68
1863	16	30	567	3	78*	21.00
1864	15	25	824	4	119	39.24
1865	21	37	788	5	110	24.63
1866	17	31	552	1	65	18.40
1867	15	27	443	2	59*	17.72
1868	18	32	516	1	79	16.64
1869	11	20	369	-	58	18.45
1870	19	35	319	5	66	10.63
1871	17	32	423	3	50	14.59
Career	**256**	**452**	**7,360**	**41**	**119**	**17.91**

Bowling averages & wicket-keeping performances in all first-class matches

	Overs	Maidens	Runs	Wickets	Average	Catches	Stumpings
1853						1	1
1854	290.3	132	352	43	8.19	2	
1855	7.1	1	15	1	15.00	2	
1856	10	3	23	1	23.00	6	
1857	232	110	359	28	12.82	14	
1858	614.2	228	988	75	13.17	8	1
1859	586.3	205	913	51	17.90	12	2
1860	137	38	238	19	12.53	8	2
1861	242.3	74	451	19	23.74	16	3
1862	246.1	59	456	20	22.80	13	5
1863	83.2	22	185	5	37.00	14	
1864	35	7	85	3	28.33	6	
1865	253	75	518	27	19.19	12	4
1866	81	8	213	8	26.62	5	2
1867	30	10	56	2	28.00	6	
1868						7	
1869	25	9	40	0		4	
1870	3	0	9	0		9	1
1871	16	2	57	0		6	4
Career	**2,893.3**	**983**	**4,958**	**302**	**16.42**	**152**	**25**

APPENDIX 2

Batting averages for Surrey in first-class matches

	Matches	Innings	Runs	Not out	Highest Score	Average
1853	1	2	13	1	8*	13.00
1854	4	7	99	1	49	14.14
1855	1	2	0	-	0	-
1856	3	4	76	-	57	19.00
1857	7	10	162	1	40*	18.00
1858	6	9	202	-	87	22.44
1859	6	11	177	-	48	16.09
1860	7	12	178	2	30	17.80
1861	11	18	187	-	42	10.39
1862	11	18	376	1	67	22.12
1863	10	18	397	1	78*	23.35
1864	10	16	483	4	119	40.25
1865	16	27	628	4	110	27.30
1866	13	24	465	-	65	19.38
1867	14	26	417	2	59*	17.38
1868	16	29	418	1	44*	14.93
1869	10	18	359	-	58	19.94
1870	17	31	295	4	66	10.93
1871	16	30	406	2	50	14.50
Career	**179**	**312**	**5,338**	**24**	**119**	**18.53**

Bowling averages and wicket-keeping performances for Surrey in first-class matches

	Overs	Maidens	Runs	Wickets	Average	Catches	Stumpings
1853						1	1
1854	183.2	90	206	27	7.63	1	
1855	4	0	12	0	-	1	
1856	10	3	23	1	23.00	2	
1857	62	29	108	8	13.50	4	
1858	368.3	129	600	44	13.64	5	
1859	311.2	93	518	20	25.90	5	
1860	100	32	170	17	10.00	3	
1861	188.2	53	349	15	23.27	8	1
1862	209.1	55	339	17	19.94	10	3
1863	66.2	17	146	3	48.67	6	
1864	29	7	57	1	57.00	5	
1865	248	74	502	27	18.59	8	1
1866	69	6	188	8	23.50	3	
1867	30	10	56	2	28.00	6	
1868						6	
1869	25	9	40	0	-	3	
1870	3	0	9	0	-	9	1
1871	2	0	15	0	-	5	4
Career	**1,910**	**607**	**3,338**	**190**	**17.57**	**91**	**11**

APPENDIX 2

Batting averages for the Players in first-class matches

	Matches	Innings	Runs	Not out	Highest Score	Average
1857	2	3	40	-	28	13.33
1858	2	4	30	1	16	10.00
1859	2	3	62	-	41	20.67
1860	1	1	10	-	10	10.00
1861	1	1	27	-	27	27.00
1862	1	2	60	1	33*	60.00
1863	1	2	5	-	5	2.50
1864	1	2	143	-	117	71.50
1865	2	4	37	-	16	9.25
1869	1	2	10	-	7	5.00
Career	**14**	**24**	**424**	**2**	**117**	**19.27**

Bowling averages and wicket-keeping performances for the Players in first-class matches

	Overs	Maidens	Runs	Wickets	Average	Catches	Stumpings
1857	30	11	66	4	16.50	2	
1858	36.2	16	62	6	10.33	1	
1859	60.3	21	94	6	15.67	2	
1860	18	3	35	1	35.00		
1862	17	2	49	0	-		
1863						3	
1864						1	
1865							1
1869						1	
Career	**162.1**	**53**	**306**	**17**	**18.00**	**10**	**1**

APPENDIX 2

Batting averages for the South of England in first-class matches

	Matches	Innings	Runs	Not out	Highest Score	Average
1854	1	2	33	-	33	16.50
1855	1	2	9	1	5*	9.00
1857	3	6	22	1	10	4.40
1858	1	2	38	1	34*	38.00
1859	1	1	9	-	9	9.00
1860	2	4	35	-	19	8.75
1861	1	2	6	-	6	3.00
1862	2	4	57	1	55*	19.00
1863	3	6	108	2	60	27.00
1864	2	4	93	-	36	23.25
1865	2	4	118	1	54	39.33
1866	1	1	13	-	13	13.00
Career	**20**	**38**	**541**	**7**	**60**	**17.45**

Bowling averages and wicket-keeping performances for the South of England in first-class matches

	Overs	Maidens	Runs	Wickets	Average	Catches	Stumpings
1854	48.2	12	81	5	16.20		
1855	3.1	1	3	1	3.00		
1857	62.3	32	63	6	10.50	1	
1858	60	26	111	5	22.20		
1859	31.2	15	49	5	9.80		
1860	12	?	16	1	16.00	2	1
1861						1	1
1862	11	2	36	2	18.00	1	1
1863						5	
1865	5	1	16	0	-	1	
1866						1	
Career	**234**	**89**	**375**	**25**	**15.00**	**12**	**3**

APPENDIX 3

5 wickets in an innings in first-class cricket

Dates	Venues	Matches	Overs	Mdns.	Runs	Wkts.
3-5 July 1854	Trent Bridge	Notts. v **Surrey**	40	18	51	6
17-19 August 1854	Hove	Sussex v **England**	18	8	22	7
18-19 June 1857	Oval	**Surrey** v Cambridgeshire	10	6	16	5
5-6 July 1858	Lord's	**England** v Kent	21.2	12	16	5
			22.3	11	28	8
22-23 July 1858	Oval	**Surrey** v England	22.1	9	34	6
			37	14	61	6
2-4 August 1858	Oval	**Surrey** v North	53.1	24	79	6
9-11 June 1859	Hove	Sussex & Kent v **Surrey**	38.2	25	31	6
27-29 June 1859	Lord's	**South** v North	25.2	13	34	5
25-26 July 1859	Lord's	M C C v **Surrey Club**	41.3	15	67	5
14-15 June 1860	Oval	**Surrey** v Notts.	30	8	38	5
23-25 August 1860	Broughton, Manchester	North v **Surrey**	36.1	14	58	7
19-20 August 1861	Oval	**Surrey** v Kent	48	15	114	5
20-21 July 1865	Oval	**Surrey** v Kent	17	8	28	5
3-5 August 1865	Oval	**Surrey** v South	38.3	8	91	6
24-25 August 1865	Southampton	Hampshire v **Surrey**	46	19	70	5

10 wickets in a match in first-class cricket

Dates	Venues	Matches	Overs	Mdns.	Runs	Wkts.
3-5 July 1854	Trent Bridge	Notts. v **Surrey**	50	24	55	10
5-6 July 1858	Lord's	**England** v Kent	44.1	23	44	13
22-23 July 1858	Oval	**Surrey** v England	59.1	23	95	12
2-4 August 1858	Oval	**Surrey** v North	91.1	38	149	10

APPENDIX 4

Batting averages for the All England Eleven in non first-class matches

	Matches	Innings	Runs	Not out	Highest Score	Average
1854	15	27	157	2	23*	6.28
1855	23	39	401	3	58	11.14
1856	17	28	243	2	28*	9.35
1857	11	16	160	2	69	11.43
1858	14	23	154	2	26	7.33
1859	4	5	36	-	21	7.20
1860	4	5	26	-	18	5.20
1861	9	14	91	3	16	8.27
1862	21	36	284	2	42	8.35
1863	12	20	136	2	28*	7.56
Career	**130**	**213**	**1,688**	**18**	**69**	**8.66**

Bowling averages and wicket-keeping performances for the All England Eleven in non first-class matches

	Overs	Runs	Wickets	Average	Catches	Stumpings
1854			133		18	3
1855	30	38	2	19.00	28	14
1856	33.2	40	9	4.44	15	9
1857	184.1	221	29	7.62	17	16
1858	438.2	521	95	5.48	17	12
1859	90	101	18	5.61	3	5
1860					2	9
1861	2	7	0	-	11	23
1862	13	12	1	12.00	39	47
1863					14	26
Career	**791.1**	**940**	**154**		**164**	**164**
			+133 wkts.			

Frederick Lillywhite's Cricket Scores and Biographies of Celebrated Cricketers, vol. IV: 1849-1854 provides a detailed bowling analysis for only two of the matches in which H H Stephenson played in 1854.

APPENDIX 4

Batting averages for the United South of England Eleven in non first-class matches

	Matches	Innings	Runs	Not out	Highest Score	Average
1864	1	2	16	-	14	8.00
1865	3	6	41	-	21	6.83
1866	8	14	75	2	41*	6.25
1867	7	10	63	1	17	7.00
1868	8	16	78	4	14	6.50
1869	6	10	96	3	42*	13.71
1870	2	4	23	1	11	7.67
1871	7	11	100	3	24*	12.50
1872		Did	not	play		
1873	3	6	68	1	34*	13.60
1874	3	6	61	-	21	12.20
1875	2	3	8	-	8	2.67
Career	**50**	**88**	**629**	**15**	**42***	**8.62**

Bowling and wicket-keeping performances for the United South of England Eleven in non first-class matches

	Wickets	Catches	Stumpings
1864		-	-
1865		2	-
1866	7	6	-
1867	10	10	1
1868		7	9
1869		2	1
1870		1	-
1871		7	9
1872	Did	not	play
1873		2	3
1874		1	7
1875		2	1
Career	**17**	**40**	**31**

M C C Cricket Scores and Biographies
do not provide bowling analyses for these games

APPENDIX 5

H H Stephenson as umpire

Umpires	Match	Venue	Date
Julius Caesar & H H	Gentlemen v Players	Kennington Oval	28-30 June 1866
E Willsher & H H	Gentlemen v Players	Kennington Oval	15-17 July 1867
L Greenwood & H H	South of England v North of England	Kennington Oval	3-4 June 1869
W Mortlock & H H	Gentlemen v Players	Kennington Oval	14-16 July 1870
E Stephenson & H H	United South of England v United North of England	Kennington Oval	22-24 August 1870
L Greenwood & H H	North of England v South of England	Dewsbury	5-6 September 1870
W Mortlock & H H	Gentlemen v Players	Kennington Oval	6-8 July 1871
G Griffith & H H	Gentlemen v Players	Kennington Oval	4-5 July 1872
C K Pullin & H H	Gloucestershire v Surrey	Cheltenham College	18-19 July 1872
T Humphrey & H H	South of England v North of England	Kennington Oval	25-26 July 1872
T Humphrey & H H	Gentlemen v Players	Kennington Oval	2-4 July 1874
W Mortlock & H H	Gentlemen v Players	Kennington Oval	1-3 July 1875
R Thoms & H H	England v Australia Test Match	Kennington Oval	6-8 September 1880
R Carpenter & H H	Cambridge University v The Australians	F P Fenner's Ground, Cambridge	29-31 May 1882

APPENDIX 6

H H Stephenson's Old Boys who were awarded their Blue for cricket at Oxford or Cambridge

Oxford

J H M Hare	1879
G R Bardswell	1894, 1896, captain 1897

Cambridge

A P Lucas	1875, 1876, 1877, 1878
W S Patterson	1875, 1876, captain 1877
D Q Steel	1876, 1877, 1878, 1879
H T Luddington	1876, 1877
S S Schultz	1877
C P Wilson	1880, 1881
J A Turner	1883, 1884, 1885, 1886
L A Orford	1886, 1887
L Martineau	1887
G MacGregor	1888, 1889, 1890, captain 1891
C E M Wilson	1895, 1896, 1897, captain 1898
W McG Hemingway	1895, 1896
T L Taylor	1898, 1899, captain 1900
A E Hind	1898, 1899, 1900, 1901
C E Winter	1902

H H Stephenson's Old Boys who played in Test Matches for England

Player	Dates	Venues	Opponents
A P Lucas (5)	1878-79	Melbourne	Australia
	1880	Kennington Oval	Australia
	1882	Kennington Oval	Australia
	1884	Old Trafford, Lord's	Australia
S S Schultz (1)	1878-79	Melbourne	Australia
S Christopherson (1)	1884	Lord's	Australia
G MacGregor (8)	1890	Lord's, Kennington Oval	Australia
	1891-92	Melbourne, Sydney, Adelaide	Australia
	1893	Lord's, Kennington Oval, Old Trafford	Australia
C E M Wilson (2)	1898-99	Johannesburg, Cape Town	South Africa

Sources

Books

Alverstone, Lord and Alcock, C W, *Surrey Cricket – its history and associations*, Longmans, Green and Co., London, 1902

Anderson, Ian G, *History of Esher*, The Wolsey Press, Esher, 1948

Bennett, P W, *A Very Definite Position*, Grosvenor Ltd., Blackpool, 1992

Bettesworth, W A, *Chats on the Cricket Field*, Merritt & Hatcher Ltd., London, 1910

Bradshaw, Ted and Shaw, Bob, *A History of Evesham Cricket Club*, Evesham Cricket Club, Evesham, 2004

Caffyn, William, *Seventy-one not out: the reminiscences of William Caffyn*, William Blackwood & Sons, Edinburgh and London, 1899

Chesterton, George and Doggart, Hubert, *Oxford and Cambridge Cricket*, Willow Books, London, 1989

Daft, Richard, *Kings of Cricket: anecdotes and reminiscences from 1858 to 1892*, Tillotson & Son, Bolton, 1893

Frith, David, *The Trailblazers: The First English Cricket Tour of Australia 1861-62*, Boundary Books, Goostrey, 1999

Graham, John P, *Forty Years of Uppingham*, Macmillan and Co., Ltd., London, 1932

Harte, Chris, *A History of Australian Cricket*, Andre Deutsch Ltd., London, 1993

Hutchins, Lisa, *Esher and Claygate Past*, Historical Publications Ltd., London, 2001

Jones, Mrs Herbert, *The Princess Charlotte of Wales*, Bernard Quaritch, London, 1885

Lemmon, David, *The Official History of Middlesex County Cricket Club*, Christopher Helm, London, 1988

Lemmon, David, *The Official History of Surrey County Cricket Club*, Christopher Helm, London, 1989

Lewis, Tony, *Double Century: The Story of M C C and Cricket*, Hodder & Stoughton, London, 1987

Lillywhite, Frederick, *The English Cricketers' Trip to Canada and the United States in 1859*, with an introduction by Robin Marlar, World's Work Ltd., Tadworth, 1980

Lillywhite, Frederick, *The Guide to Cricketers*, Eighth Edition, Frederick Lillywhite, London, 1855

Lillywhite, John, *John Lillywhite's Cricketers' Companion*, John Lillywhite, London, 1871

Major, John, *More than a Game*, HarperCollins*Publishers*, London, 2007

Matthews, Bryan, *The Book of Rutland*, Barracuda Books Ltd., Buckingham, 1978

Moyes, A G, *Australian Cricket: a History*, Angus & Robertson Ltd., Sydney and Melbourne, 1959

Parkin, G R, *Life and Letters of Edward Thring*, Macmillan & Co. Ltd., London, 1900

Patterson, William S, *Sixty Years of Uppingham Cricket*, Longmans, Green and Co., London, 1909

Pycroft, James, *The Cricket-Field, with some Notes by H H Stephenson*, ed. F S Ashley-Cooper, St James's Press Co. Ltd., London, 1922

Ranjitsinhji, K S, *The Jubilee Book of Cricket*, William Blackwood & Sons, Edinburgh and London, 1897

Richardson, Nigel, *Typhoid in Uppingham: Analysis of a Victorian Town and School in Crisis 1875-1877*, Pickering & Chatto, London, 2008

Warner, Sir Pelham, *Gentlemen v Players 1806-1949*, George G Harrap & Co. Ltd., London, 1950

Webber, J R, *The Chronicle of W G*, Association of Cricket Statisticians and Historians, West Bridgford, 1998

Wynne-Thomas, Peter, *George Parr*, Famous Cricketers Series: No.20, Association of Cricket Statisticians and Historians, West Bridgford, 1993

Wynne-Thomas, Peter, *Trent Bridge – A History of the Ground to commemorate the 150th Anniversary 1838-1988*, Nottinghamshire County Council, Nottingham, 1987

Directories

Austin, K A, 'Devine, Edward (1833-1908)' in *Australian Dictionary of Biography*, 1972, Online Edition

Bailey, Philip; Thorn, Philip and Wynne-Thomas, Peter, *Who's Who of Cricketers*, Hamlyn, London, 1992

C N Wright's Directory of Leicestershire and Rutland, 1896, Tompkin and Shardlow, Leicester, 1896

Frederick Lillywhite's Cricket Scores and Biographies of Celebrated Cricketers, vols. III-IV: 1841-1854, Frederick Lillywhite, London, 1863

Frindall, Bill, ed. *The Wisden Book of Cricket Records*, Queen Anne Press, 1986

Frindall, Bill, *England Test Cricketers*, Willow Books, London, 1989

Hawthorn's Uppingham Almanack for 1893

International Genealogical Index Website

John Lillywhite's Cricket Annual for 1873, London, 1874

Kelly's Directory of Leicestershire and Rutland, 1881, Kelly & Co., London, 1881

Kelly's Directory of Worcestershire, 1860, Kelly & Co., London, 1860

M C C Cricket Scores and Biographies, vols. V-IX: 1855-66, Longmans & Co., London, 1876-7

The Doings of the Uppingham Rovers, vol. I

Uppingham Parish Church Churchwardens Account Book, 1871-1939

Uppingham Register of Land Values, 1879

Uppingham School Roll, 1824-1894, Edward Stanford, London, 1894

Journals, Magazines and Newspapers

Baily's Magazine of Sports and Pastimes, A H Baily & Co., London, 1861

Bell's Life in London and Sporting Chronicle, 9 July 1854

Hornung, E W, 'Our Public Schools: XVI – Uppingham' in *Country Life*, 28 July 1917

Martineau, G D, 'A Hat-Trick Centenary?' in *The Cricketer*: Spring Annual, London, 1958

Sheffield and Rotherham Independent, 11 September 1858

Supplement to the Uppingham School Magazine, October 1890

The Cricket Field, 1 June 1895

The Evesham Journal, 23 and 30 March, 18 May and 21 December 1861; 28 March 1863; 11 November 1865; 7 July 1866; 11 December 1869 and 18 March 1871

The Hull and Eastern Counties Herald, 16 July 1874

The Lincoln, Rutland and Stamford Mercury, 2 August 1872; 18 July 1873; 22 February 1878; 30 May 1879; 13 May 1881; 26 March 1886; 4 April 1890 and 25 December 1896

The Sunday Times, 31 August and 19 October 1845

The Times, 23 March 1848 and 5 April 1865

Tozer, Malcolm, 'The First of the Great School Coaches' in *The Journal of the Cricket Society*, vol. XVII: Autumn, London, 1994

Uppingham School Magazine, September 1864; March and November 1874; June 1878; April 1883 and March 1898

Written communication and manuscripts
(all material in the collection of John Oakley, unless otherwise stated)

Census Returns, 1841-1891, Record Office for Leicestershire, Leicester and Rutland, Wigston Magna; Surrey History Centre, Woking

Draft of an undated letter from H H to Henry Perkins, Secretary of the M C C

General Registers of Births, Marriages and Deaths, General Register Office, Southport

Invitation to the wedding of Princesse Marguerite d'Orléans

Letter from Catherine Stephenson to H H, undated

Letter from Dr H E Platt to 'My Dear H H', 20 July 1895

Letter from M Willbe Stephenson to 'My dear Frances', 19 May 1918

Letter from William S Patterson to Mrs Stephenson, 18 December 1896

Letters from H H to daughter Frances, 25 December 1889 and 1893

Minutes of a committee meeting of the Surrey County Cricket Club, 28 April 1853, Surrey History Centre, Woking

Passport document issued to H H, Foreign Office, London, 3 November 1871

INDEX
Page references in italics indicate a photograph or illustration